POMPEII IN FACT AND FICTION

Pompeii
in Fact and Fiction

WOLFGANG LEPPMANN

ELEK BOOKS LIMITED

ALL SAINTS STREET LONDON

© 1966 Nymphenburger Verlagshandlung GmbH, München

All rights reserved

Published in 1968 by
ELEK BOOKS LIMITED
2 All Saints Street London N 1

and simultaneously in Canada by
THE RYERSON PRESS
299 Queen Street West Toronto 2B

Originally published under the title
Pompeji: Eine Stadt in Literatur und Leben

Printed in the Republic of Ireland by
HELY THOM LIMITED, DUBLIN

Contents

List of Illustrations

The Publishers would like to acknowledge the photographs to the following sources:

Bruckmann Verlag, Munich: 1, 2b, 3, 7, 16b; Archiv fur Kunst und Geschichte, Berlin: 2a, 6a; Edwin Smith: 4a, 4b, 14b; F. Alinari, Florence: 5, 9, 10, 15; Reproduced by courtesy of the Trustees, The National Gallery, London: 11; Nymphenburger Verlag, Munich: 8a; reproduced by courtesy of the Trustees of the British Museum, London: 8b, 16a; Biblioteca Governativa, Cremona: 12; Musei Vaticani, Rome: 13; Reproduced by courtesy of the Trustees of the National Portrait Gallery, London: 6b; Hans Edwards: 14a.

Acknowledgements

Apart from the titles listed in the bibliography at the end of the book, the following have proved very useful in the preparation of this study: A. Sogliano, *Pompeii nella letteratura* (Naples, 1888); S. Herrlich, *Die antike Überlieferung über den Vesuv-Ausbruch im Jahre 79* (Leipzig, 1904); and F. F. Murga, *Pompeya en la literatura española* (Naples, 1965).—While indebtedness to others has been indicated in the footnotes, the author has reason to acknowledge, specifically and gratefully, the help he has received from the late Amedeo Maiuri, *Soprintendente alle Antichità della Campania*, and his successor Alfonso de Franciscis; from C. B. Beall and F. M. Combellack of Eugene, Oregon; Ruth Kromer of Anacapri; F. Fernández Murga of the *Instituto Español de Santiago en Nápoles;* F. Martini of Stuttgart; W. Ross of Munich; and the John Simon Guggenheim Foundation. Translations are mine unless otherwise noted.

Wolfgang Leppmann
Eugene, Oregon
Summer 1966

A Note on Pompeiian Topography

Although topographical indications have been held to a minimum, it is well to point out that the city is divided into nine sections or *regiones*, numbered counterclockwise from the Stabian Gate. The *regiones* in turn are subdivided, by the side streets running off the main thorough-fares (the *decumanus major* or Strada dell'Abbondanza, the *decumanus minor* or Via di Nola, and the *cardo* or Via di Stabia), into *insulae* or blocks. Individual houses within each block are numbered, and occasionally named as well—after the owner (House of Loreius Tiburtinus), after a particular architectural feature (House of the Lararium) or work of art (House of the Golden Cupids), after a distinguished visitor (House of Queen Margherita) or event (House of the Silver Wedding, discovered in 1893 when that anniversary was celebrated in the Italian Royal Family), or after a combination of these (House of the Faun—House of Goethe—House of the Battle of Alexander).

Foreword

THE DRAMATIC destruction of Pompeii and Herculaneum, and their gradual but no less dramatic resurrection during the past two-and-a-half centuries, are major events in cultural history. The porcelain of Josiah Wedgwood and of his competitors in Sèvres and Dresden, the paintings of Ingres and David, the architecture of Neoclassicism and the fashions and furniture of the Empire are no less indebted to Pompeii than were Heinrich Schliemann, who might never have set out to find Troy without the example of this previously excavated city before his eyes, Sigmund Freud, whose interest in the psychoanalytical interpretation of literature was awakened by a novel set in Pompeii, and Friedrich Nietzsche, who encapsulated his many exhortations to those who should lead exposed and therefore heightened lives into the command 'Build your houses by Vesuvius!' Without Pompeii, the ancient city which has been investigated longer and more thoroughly than any other, we would know very little about daily life in classical times; without Vesuvius, the volcano which has been observed longer and more thoroughly than any other, our knowledge of the physical universe would be substantially reduced. Who can say how different the world might be if this little country town, along with its still more insignificant neighbour Herculaneum, had not been buried, preserved, and by mere chance rediscovered after almost seventeen centuries? Entire disciplines like epigraphy, geology, and above all archaeology would have developed along different lines; so would sculpture, painting, and—literature.

'There are moments in human life,' August von Kotzebue wrote in 1805, 'which have a stamp of distinction on them above all the rest: they form no part of the common chain of recollections which occupy our minds; they ever retain their original brightness, unclouded by any of the mists and darkness of time; they are the last objects on which the eye dwells when ready to close forever . . . Such has Pompeii afforded to me . . . What I saw there in a few hours will often, in calm retrospect, withdraw my mind from the world around me.' Whether they wrote at length or contented themselves with a brief remark like Stendhal's '*Ce que j'ai vu de plus curieux dans mon voyage, c'est Pompéia*' —the most disparate authors have been deeply affected by what they saw in Pompeii, and for good reason; for here, more than anywhere else on earth, are activated two of the strongest of human concerns: the existential concern with man's fate and the cultural concern with man's past. This fascination with Pompeii has found expression in a variety of literary forms, in travel books like Mark Twain's *Innocents Abroad*, operas like Béraud's *Les ruines de Pompéia*, works of fiction like Bulwer-Lytton's celebrated story, exchanges of correspondence such as those between Walpole and West or Shelley and Peacock, short stories like Malcolm Lowry's *Present Estate of Pompeii*, scientific essays like Freud's *Der Wahn und die Träume in W. Jensens 'Gradiva'*, novels like Madame de Staël's *Corinne*, autobiographical works like Goethe's *Italienische Reise*, poems like Leopardi's *La Ginestra*. If this large and variegated body of writing extends over much of the spectrum of artistic expression, its spatial and temporal range is equally impressive; it encompasses several national literatures from the early Roman Empire to the mid-twentieth century.

Given the lack of examples which might be followed in writing the literary biography of a city (a task very different from that of compiling a city chronicle or a *Motivgeschichte*), our methodological scaffold will have to be improvised and consist of the Life-and-Works of this or that author, the relevant cultural and historical co-ordinates, and the occasional retelling and analysis of a story or poem; and even though it is sometimes assumed that fun and learning do not mix, we will not go out of our way to avoid the odd anecdote as long as it is meaningful and authenticated. An insight into works more or less centred on Pompeii seems more useful in this context than a listing, for the sake of completeness alone, of others in which the city plays only a peripheral role as it does in Stifter's *Brigitta*, Raabe's *Altershausen*, or Montale's *Sarcofaghi*. Avoiding all technical language, we will examine this 'Pompeiian' writing, quote from it on occasion, set it off against the historical background, and wherever possible lay bare the biographical and artistic phase in which the writer under discussion discovered this motif, transformed it in his mind, and released it as a work of literature.

Seen in this light, the literary history of Pompeii is remarkable not only because the city often inspired writers to works of extraordinary stature, so that Pliny wrote the two best letters, Leopardi the greatest poem, and Bulwer-Lytton the most successful novel of his life, but also because this theme, polarized between life and death, has become doubly significant in our age which is so apocalyptic in nature and yet so averse to metaphysical reasoning. Far from being dismissed as remnant of an outlived humanistic culture, the Pompeiian motif has been reawakened to new life precisely in the works of Hartlaub, Peyrefitte, Del Valle, Lowry, and other quasi-contemporaries. In the course of this development, the literature on Pompeii has come to represent not only a collection of writings, but a touchstone of writing.

Wolfgang Leppmann

I
Pompeii in the Ancient World

'cuncta iacent flammis et tristi mersa favilla: nec superi vellent hoc licuisse sibi.'

All lies buried in flames and melancholy ashes; the Gods themselves may wish that this had not been permitted to them . . .

Martial, Epigram IV, 44

WE DO NOT know exactly when Pompeii was first settled. The oldest building which can be identified and reconstructed from its ruins, the Doric Temple in the Triangular Forum, dates from the sixth century B.C.; but there are no inscriptions, literary documents, or architectural remains to indicate how long the site had been inhabited at that time. Nor do the legends which have immortalized so many localities along the magic shore of Campania throw much light on Pompeii. Just below the southern edge of the crescent-shaped bay of Naples lie the Isole Sirenuse or Li Galli; these rocks, now the property of the choreographer Léonide Massine, were thought by the ancients to be the islands into which the sirens were metamorphosed after they had swum in pursuit of Ulysses' ship and vainly enticed him to land. The most seductive of these nymphs, Parthenope, lent her name to the Greek settlement from which the city of Naples was to evolve. A stone's throw from the Naples waterfront lies the island of Megaris, a speck of land which brackets, as it were, classical antiquity from its mythological beginnings to its historical end; for here, where the Castel dell'Ovo now rises, legend has placed the grave of one of Hercules' wives as well as that of the last Roman emperor, Romulus Augustulus. At the northern extremity of the bay are found Cumae, home of the Sibyl, and the Phlegraean or Burning Fields on which the Olympian Gods vanquished the giants (and in order to keep them subdued, buried them under boulders and mountains which stir, in the earthquakes characteristic of the region, whenever the imprisoned monsters try to shake them off). Further north yet are Capua and Gaeta, said to have been founded by that prolific father of cities, Aeneas of Troy. Hercules himself lives on in Herculaneum, linked to Pompeii by a kindred fate; but although the Doric Temple was at one time dedicated to him, the hero's connection with Pompeii itself remains somewhat tenuous. It almost seems as if this city, known above all others by the spectacular manner of its death, had purposely eschewed any poetic elaboration of its birth.

If it remains uncertain *when* Pompeii was settled, there can be little doubt as to *why* it was settled. During a prehistoric eruption of Mount Vesuvius, a tongue of lava, flowing in a south-easterly direction, had come to stop at the mouth of the Sarno River not far from the shore. In the course of time it cooled and formed a knoll affording a wide view of land and sea, with ample warning of an enemy approaching from any side. This strategic advantage was soon enhanced by an economic one: the town lies on the trade route leading to Salerno and down to Reggio Calabria, at the toe of the Italian boot where Sicily is within sight and easy reach. At Pompeii, another and much shorter road branches off; passing through Castellammare di Stabia, it leads to Sorrento and the promontory facing Capri. Situated practically on the seashore, which a series of later eruptions was to push back, and on the Sarno which was navigable for the shallow-draughted vessels of antiquity, the settlement soon became a trans-shipment point for the Phoenician and Greek traders who exported the produce of Campania. The mild climate and volcanic soil of this region favoured the cultivation of grapes, apples, pears, quinces, figs, almonds, melons, and cherries, as well as hemp, grain, and the tall, thin-stalked cabbage for which Pompeii was famous. The sea, equally generous, teemed with a variety of fish from which the ancients made *garum*, a spicy sauce which was likewise a local specialty. The woods were full of game down to the times of that royal Nimrod, Ferdinand IV of the Two Sicilies, and the very earth contained not only tufa but the particular Vesuvian lava which the Elder Cato recommended as suitable for millstones. In short, the ancients must have considered the situation of Pompeii as desirable economically as the modern traveller finds it enviable on account of its charm. It is probably due to its natural endowment, rather than to any ethnic or characteristic peculiarity of its inhabitants (who, all in all, seem to have been a somewhat undistinguished lot), that Pompeii came to acquire that mercantile aspect which sets it apart, even in its ruins, from such cities as Knossos, Athens, Sparta, Rome, and Palmyra, whose function and 'image' were hieratic, military, and administrative rather than commercial. It is surely no coincidence that pride of possession, and the desire to hold on to one's acquisitions, should have motivated the famous inscriptions CAVE CANEM and SALVE LUCRUM. 'Beware of the dog' and 'Welcome, profits!'—these sentiments may well have been as characteristically Pompeiian as the expression on the bust of the banker L. Caecilius Jucundus.

Pompeii had the good fortune of lying at a cultural as well as a commercial crossroads. When it was founded, somewhere in the period 850 to 650 B.C., Italy was inhabited by three major ethnic groups. If their respective spheres of influence were to be represented graphically, the town would be found to lie at the point where they touched. Under the impact of the Doric migration, the Eolian and Ionian Greeks had begun to send colonists to various parts of the Mediterranean littoral. One of the earliest of these colonies was Cumae, founded about 900 B.C. by Ionians from Euboae; it was soon followed by the neighbouring centres of Dicearcheia (Pozzuoli), Parthenope and Palaeopolis (Naples), and a little farther to the South, Poseidonia (Paestum). Although the Greek settlements eventually extended to the southern coasts of France and Spain, the Bay of Naples marked for all practical purposes the outer rim of what came to be called *Magna Graecia* or Greece Beyond the Sea. Only in Sicily did the Greeks penetrate inland; by and large, they were more concerned with safeguarding the lines of communication with their home bases than with colonizing, pioneer-fashion, the mountainous regions of the interior.

In the southern and central part of the peninsula, this hinterland was inhabited by the Italic tribes, which shared with the Greeks a common Indo-european heritage but had failed to reach a comparable level of development. Their agrarian way of life is still reflected in such place names as Bovianum or 'Oxtown', the capital of the Samnites, and possibly the word 'Italy' itself, which may have derived from Oscan *vitaliù* (calf, veal). However, their rudimentary social organization and undeveloped sense of cohesion did not allow them to found any cities which could compete with the Greek *poleis*. These early Italians were herdsmen who produced at home what little they needed by way of food, clothing, tools, and arms.

Between the Samnites, Oscans, Lucanians, and other southern tribes and their cousins to the North, the Ligures and Veneti, lived the third and at the time most powerful ethnic group: the Etruscans. Like the Greeks, they were not indigenous to Italy but had immigrated; it is still not known with any certainty when, whence, or even by what means. They had settled in what is now Tuscany and in some adjacent regions of north-central Italy; for a time they also ruled over Campania, at least as far south as Capua and almost certainly as far as Pompeii. Although their language, their art, and in particular their religion, with its divination of the future by especially appointed priests which was to be copied by the Romans, differed radically from those of the Greeks, they had developed along similar lines and reached a comparable degree of political, social, and artistic articulation. In contrast to the Italic tribes, the Greeks and Etruscans had maritime and commercial skills. They were gifted with a strong awareness of their own national and racial individuality, and tended to congregate in cities rather than live scattered in the open country; while the few settlements established by the Italic tribes have disappeared from history, those founded by the Etruscans—Arezzo, Perugia, Florence, and in all likelihood Rome— have survived the centuries as gallantly as did the cities of *Magna Graecia:* Taranto, Messina, Syracuse, Naples. For us, the characteristic note introduced into Italy by these foreigners is most clearly expressed in their art. At first sight, the tombs of Cerveteri and Tarquinia differ greatly from the temples of Paestum, and the statuary in the Museum of Villa Giulia from the bronze Ephebus found in Pompeii; yet they are equally far removed, in originality and technical skill, from the un- inspired pottery found in the Samnite museums of such towns as Benevento and Lecce.

Not much is known of the history of Pompeii in ancient times, and our needs are in any case adequately served by a very brief survey. Soon after its foundation by the Oscans (who seem to have given the town its name, perhaps derived from *pompe* meaning 'five'), it fell under the domination of the Greeks from Cumae, and, probably, of the Etruscans. The rectangular layout of the oldest section, the design of the original city wall, and some family names such as that of the Cuspii are thought to be of Etruscan origin. This influence, however, must have been of short duration, for the Greeks defeated the Etruscans in two battles fought near Cumae, in 524 and 474 B.C., putting an end to their rule in Campania; so rapid was the decline in their power that between these dates, the Etruscan kings were also chased out of Rome. Eventually, the expanding Roman Republic interposed itself between the Etruscan homeland to the North and its extension in the Bay of Naples; deprived of a land connection, the southern settlements were left to wither on the vine. About 420 B.C., when the Greeks were absorbed by the fratricidal Peloponnesian War, the Samnites descended from their hills and occupied the Osco-Grecian settlements on the shore, including Pompeii which may then have had some 3,000 inhabitants. Hardier than the Oscans, and not subjected, as these had been for centuries, to the enervating if civilizing influence of Greek culture, the Samnites imposed upon the town their own language, customs, and civic institutions. They rebuilt and enlarged the fortifications constructed by their predecessors, and maintained their dominion over Pompeii even while they were themselves gradually being conquered by the Romans, in a drawn-out process during which alliances between the two peoples alternated with sanguinary conflicts. These are usually grouped together as the Samnite Wars (343–290 B.C.) and comprise a number of later passages-at-arms as well, in which the Samnite Confederation, alone or with such partners as the Etruscans, the Tarentines, Pyrrhus of Epirus, and Hannibal, endeavoured to contain the southward march of Rome.

The first episode in Pompeiian history of which we have certain knowledge took place toward the end of the Second Samnite War, at a date variously given as 310 or 302 B.C., when a marauding Roman fleet landed at the mouth of the Sarno, sacked the nearby town of Nuceria (Salerno), and hurriedly withdrew when the local populace rose up in arms. The Romans, however, were not to be put off indefinitely. They occupied Naples as early as 326 B.C., and in all likelihood took (at first perhaps only temporary) possession of Pompeii a few decades later. During the next two centuries, in any event, Roman rule appears to have been a matter of form rather than substance. The town lay within the area effectively controlled by the Romans, but its inhabitants were virtually independent and even took part in several coalitions against their overlords. When Hannibal had annihilated the Roman army at Cannae, in 216, the Pompeiians, joining the Campanian Greeks and the Samnites, went over to the Carthaginian side; but already the following year, the Romans defeated the invader at Nola and forced him to withdraw from the region. Unlike Capua, which had also opened its gates to Hannibal, Pompeii does not seem to have been punished for its lapse of loyalty.

A century and a few years later, the Samnites, Piceni, and other Italic peoples, realizing that the Roman citizenship they had been promised was being withheld and that their lands were being confiscated by the senatorial oligarchy of Rome, took up arms against the Republic in the Social War of 90–88 B.C. Pompeii found itself besieged for the better part of a year, and although it had no martial traditions of its own, the little town defended itself valiantly; the marks left by Roman projectiles can be seen to this day on the city wall between the Vesuvian and the Herculanean Gates. This protracted defence is the more remarkable as the attacking army was commanded by Lucius Cornelius Sulla, the one-time playboy who defeated the great Marius and eventually held in his hands more power than any other Roman citizen in the centuries between Tarquinius Superbus and Julius Caesar. Yet once again, the Pompeiians escaped the victor's wrath and even profited commercially from the destruction of neighbouring Stabiae. Their town was merely garrisoned by veterans of Sulla's army, many of whom settled there on being demobilized. A third of the municipal lands had been set aside for them, and it was inevitable that some friction should develop between these newcomers and the old residents; in one of his orations, Cicero had to defend the dictator's nephew, P. Cornelius Sulla, against the charge of fomenting discord and inciting the citizens to join the Catilinian conspiracy.

Once the Social War had ended with the gradual enfranchisement of all Italians, Pompeii sank back into the near-anonymity of provincial life. As a token of Romanization it was now called *Colonia Cornelia Veneria Pompeiianorum*, after the clan name of its conqueror L. Cornelius Sulla and the Venus Pompeiiana, whose patronage of the

city is celebrated in Statius' lament of the fate which eventually over-
took '*Veneri plorata domus*'.[1] The Osco-Samnite dialect of the people
gave way to Latin; Roman currency, weights, and measures were
introduced, and Roman forms of civil government instituted with the
establishment of a magistrate modelled on the Roman senate. As in the
capital, city officials were paid little or nothing for their work. In order
to maintain their standing with the electorate, they had to finance out
of their own pockets not only circuses and other mass entertainments,
but the construction of entire public buildings. They were accordingly
required to produce proof of independent means before presenting
themselves to the voters, who seem to have included all adult citizens
either individually or voting in corporations, as goldsmiths, worshippers
of the goddess Isis, barbers, etc. The candidates engaged in a great deal
of electioneering, and many of the graffiti or wall inscriptions found in
the ruins refer to the last civic election held before the disaster, in
March A.D. 79. Next to making money, municipal politics appear to
have been the great pastime of the ancient Pompeiians. In view of the
many inscriptions urging the electorate to vote for such-and-such a
candidate, who was usually praised as 'D.R.P.' (*dignus rei publicae* or
worthy of public office), one can sympathize with Cicero's jesting
observation that it was easier for a man to become senator in Rome
than a decurion in Pompeii.

Our knowledge of daily life in the ancient world is based to such an
extent on what has been found in Pompeii that we must guard against
generalizing from these discoveries and exaggerating the town's importance within the Roman Empire as a whole. To be sure, Pompeii
had its 'first families', such as the Popidii and Vettii; but their names
carried no weight in Rome or even Naples. If a man of real influence
ever grew up within its walls, history has not preserved his name or the
fact of his connection with Pompeii. Despite its siege during the Social
War and the brief resistance which Spartacus later put up on Mount
Vesuvius, Pompeii played no appreciable role in Roman history. It
possessed neither the macabre distinction of having witnessed a great
battle like Cannae or Pharsalus, nor the joyful one of having produced a
great poet who might have celebrated it as Catullus sang of Sirmio or
Ovid of Sulmo and even of Tomi, the bleak island of his exile. Pompeii

lives on not because it *did*, but because it *suffered* something remarkable. At the time of its destruction, it counted no more than 25,000 inhabitants, most of whom were engaged in the cultivation, manufacture, and distribution of a very limited number of products: wine, fish sauce, fruit, tufa. Because of the vagaries of archaeological discovery, much is known about certain Pompeiian trades and professions—that of the bakers, of the wool merchants, and of the meat and produce dealers who did business in the *macellum* on the Forum—and almost nothing about some others of possibly greater scope; for example, we have almost no idea of the implements used by the highly skilled plumbers who laid the city's water pipes. By the same token, the aura of wickedness which surrounds Pompeii with the *lupanare*, the initiation rites shown in the Villa of the Mysteries, and the phallic statuettes and amulets kept under lock and key in the Museo Nazionale in Naples, has given rise to the belief that the town must have been Sodom, Gomorrha, and Babylon rolled into one (a belief fomented, as we shall see, by some writers whose work will be examined in these pages). It is true that Pompeii lies on the *littora quae fuerunt inimica castis puellis*, but so do Capri and Baiae, and it is possible that our impression of the private sphere of Pompeiian life is quite one-sided. In all probability, the inhabitants of Pompeii and Herculaneum, far from being exceptionally profligate, were as representative of Roman culture in general as the inhabitants of Hiroshima and Nagasaki were of Japanese culture as a whole. It is in any case well to remember that what slight role Pompeii played in antiquity was due less to anything its citizens did or left undone, than to the fact that a number of distinguished outsiders like Cicero, Petronius' fictional Trimalchio, and several members of the Julian dynasty owned country houses there, *pompeiiana* to which they retired for their holidays.

It is not our task to give an account of life in ancient Pompeii, or to provide yet another description of the typical Roman house with its *atrium* and *triclinium*, or to enumerate the frescoes and mosaics which brightened many of these edifices. Our concern is not with the archaeological reality of Pompeii, but with the impact of the city's strange fate on the writers who visited it afterwards. We must now leave the

Pompeiians to that fate, and turn our attention to the mountain which was responsible for it.

Geologists believe that Mount Vesuvius is a volcano of subterranean and relatively recent origin (Quaternary Period), which first formed an island and later came to be joined to the spurs of the Apennine range. It belongs to the volcanic system, partly active and in part extinct, which extends along the Tyrrhenian coast from Tuscany's Monte Amiata through Capri, Stromboli, and Etna down to the island of Pantelleria between Sicily and Africa. Vesuvius itself consists of two concentric cones; Monte Somma, the outer and much older one—or rather, the north-eastern part of its rim which is still standing, the rest having collapsed in the course of time—now rises some 3,600 feet above sea level. It has been estimated that if the entire cone had been preserved, its elevation would reach 10,000 feet. In all probability, Monte Somma represents what is left of the mountain which the ancients called *Vesuvius mons*. When two distinct peaks had formed sometime after the eruption of A.D. 79, the name Vesuvius seems to have been transferred to the inner or active cone while the outer one came to be called Monte Somma. Some scientists maintain that there were two separate cones even before A.D. 79, but the weight of cultural if not geological evidence is all on the side of those who believe that the inner cone developed during and after the eruption of that year. None of the ancient writers, for example, makes a distinction between Somma and Vesuvius, and such pictures as have come down to us from classical times show only one peak, whose remains correspond to the present Somma. This is how the mountain appears on a fresco found 1779 in Herculaneum (it has since been lost, but engravings have survived in an eighteenth-century publication) and on the famous painting discovered in Pompeii a hundred years later, which depicts the god Bacchus, to whom Vesuvius was sacred, standing to the left of the mountain whose one, decidedly cone-shaped peak is covered with vines.

The great amount of lava ejected by Vesuvius in early times and the distance it flowed, to Pompeii and beyond, indicate that there must have been repeated and violent eruptions long before A.D. 79. It is probable that the volcano was even then subject to a cyclical pattern of activity in which an eruption, usually accompanied by considerable flow of lava and the destruction of the peak, is followed by a quiescent phase marked by a steady escape of gases, until a new *bocca* or mouth opens in the crater floor. The accumulation of cinders and lava issuing from this opening brings about the formation of a new cone, whose internal tensions eventually cause the wall to weaken and lava to stream out of the fissures. The sudden release of pressure, in turn, brings about the collapse of the cone, whose materials are then ejected or 'erupted' from the crater by the force of the liberated gases. In modern times, the length of such cycles has varied from a few years to a half-century, with an average of perhaps twenty-five years.

Oddly enough, the Romans before A.D. 79 do not seem to have had any notion of the volcano's continuing life (perhaps because its signs were irregular and largely subterranean). Lucretius Carus mentions the existence of hot springs near Vesuvius; Vitruvius Pollio reports that in the dim past, the mountain had rained fire on the surrounding countryside; and Diodorus Siculus, in his account of the legendary battle between Hercules and the giants, adds that Vesuvius once was an active volcano much like Etna. In the first few years of the Christian era, the most qualified of these early observers, the geographer Strabo, wrote that 'in earlier times this district was on fire and had craters of fire, and then, because the fuel gave out, was quenched'.[2] This view, based in Strabo's case on an actual ascent of the mountain, seems to have been universally held. Even the great earthquake of A.D. 63, now considered to have been a kind of dress rehearsal for the eruption of A.D. 79, or an attempt of the volcano to free itself of the pressures relentlessly building up in its cone, does not appear to have awakened any lasting apprehension that the mountain might once more burst forth in fury. Taking it as the starting point for an analysis of earthquakes in general, Seneca describes this tremor in some detail. He expresses dismay at the thought that it should have taken place in winter (the date has been established as February 5), when, 'according to the experience of our ancestors', earthquakes do not normally occur, and altogether looks at the event with a scientist's observant eye.[3] But he draws no warning from it, and when the eruption of A.D. 79 did overwhelm Pompeii and Herculaneum, he was no longer alive.

It is ironical that the volcano which fascinated the ancients should have been not Vesuvius but Etna. When Silius Italicus wanted to impress on his readers the violence of the catastrophe which had overtaken the Campanian cities, he could think of no more telling comparison than to say that 'the discharge of stones seeks to rival the death dealt by Etna'[4]—an instance of double poetic licence, because Etna had long been quiescent and the mountain which the poet sought to describe was, in any case, Vesuvius not as it looked in his own time but as it may have appeared centuries before, during the Second Punic War. In an analogy to the legend of the Phlegraean Fields and a similar tradition connected with Ischia's Monte Epomeo, Virgil mentions that Enceladus, held captive under Etna, made that volcano potentially dangerous,[5] and the anonymous author of a didactic work on volcanic phenomena similarly entitled the result of his labours, a tedious poem in hexameters which dates from the early Empire, not '*Vesuvius*' but '*Aetna*'. He disdainfully dismisses the mythological interpretation as an '*impia fabula*' and reports in passing that the upheavals triggered by Vesuvius are a thing of the past. More than a thousand years later, Boccaccio could still refer to Vesuvius as the '*imitatore dei fuochi di Etna*'; it may be argued that from a literary point of view, our volcano did not come into his own until Dumas *père* wrote:

'It must be admitted that [Vesuvius] revealed itself to the world by a master stroke. To cover land and sea with a black cloud; to send its ashes as far afield as Africa, Syria, and Egypt; to bury two cities like Pompeii and Herculaneum; to asphyxiate, over a distance of a mile, a philosopher like Pliny, and to have his nephew record the catastrophe by means of an immortal letter—you will grant that this is not bad at all for a volcano that is only just setting out on its career . . .'[6]

Despite the comforting belief held by the ancients, there is archaeological as well as geological evidence that Vesuvius had been active not only before A.D. 79, but well within the historical period. In 1902, graves dating from the eighth century B.C. were found at Striano, San Valentino, and other localities east of the crater. They were covered by two separate strata of lapilli (small pumice stones), ashes, and earth, and contained graves of Roman origin in the upper layer. These had evidently been dug by men who did not know, or had chosen to ignore, the fact that this region had been buried by Vesuvius during an earlier eruption in what must have been, to them, the relatively recent past.

As if to atone for their earlier neglect, the people of Campania have never again overlooked Vesuvius or assumed it to be harmless. At present, the mountain is under continuous observation by the staff of several scientific institutes located in the immediate neighbourhood. In earlier times, it fascinated not only scientists but also the innumerable laymen who scaled its heights and left descriptions, sketches, and paintings of what they saw. In the remoter past, in the Middle Ages when the spirit of scientific investigation had not yet begun to agitate the minds of men, travellers took pains to transmit to posterity an amount of geological information which is impressive in the aggregate. The year 685, for example, is not one which readily brings to mind many important events; but among the few things recorded as having occurred that year is an eruption of Vesuvius, in February and early March, which was accompanied by earth tremors, a heavy precipitation of ashes, and appreciable emission of lava. The sum total of such observations made in the course of the past nineteen centuries, checked against and complemented by the exact seismographic analyses of the Osservatorio Vesuviano since its foundation in 1845, enable the modern geologist to reconstruct with reasonable accuracy the chain of events which led to the destruction of Pompeii and Herculaneum. The history of Vesuvius is thus bound up with the history of vulcanology as such; in measure as this science has developed from the days of Strabo to those of Mercalli and Alfano, the volcano on which so many of its practitioners were trained has preserved its majesty but lost much of its mystery.

The eruption of A.D. 79 is, at any rate, the first historically documented event of this nature and altogether the oldest realistic description, in Western literature, of a major natural disaster. Although we are here primarily concerned with the literary aspects of the Pompeiian motif, we must keep in mind that it was not the classicists, geologists, or art historians, but the archaeologists who uncovered the site and solved some of the most puzzling problems arising from the city's destruction—in a dynamic rather than antiquarian form of research in which the position, shape, and condition of bodies and objects assume a fascination quite distinct from their cultural and artistic value. It has for example been established that the rain of ashes and lapilli fell hot enough to char and carbonize all living things, but not so hot as to set off a general conflagration: the lead pipes of the water supply did not melt, marble did not undergo calcination, and clothing was not burned off bodies.

The question as to the extent to which Pompeii and Herculaneum were destroyed by fire rather than earthquake and precipitation from the volcanic cloud is among those touched upon, but not wholly explained in the most important of the literary sources on the Great Eruption: the letters of Pliny the Younger. They are based on the author's own observations, although these were made from Misenum, some twenty miles away, and not written down in definitive form until many years after the event. Pliny had made some notes at the time, but he did not really set pen to paper, or stylus to papyrus, until his friend Cornelius Tacitus, about to collect material for his *Histories*, asked him what he remembered about the catastrophe which he happened to have witnessed in his youth. Since Tacitus' description has been lost, as has all that part of his work which dealt with events after the year A.D. 70, we have to rely on Pliny quite as much as did the historian himself. This set of circumstances, which may well be unique in the annals of literature, entitles us to an intriguing question: how much would we know about this major historical event, the disappearance of the Campanian cities beneath the ashes of Mount Vesuvius, if Pliny had died in the interval between A.D. 79 and A.D. 106, the presumed date of his letters? During all that time he was, as it turned out, posterity's only direct informant on the calamity. Without his report, the fate of Pompeii and Herculaneum might well have been transmitted to us as an historical oddity like the Asiatic origin of the Etruscans or the Viking discovery of America: not altogether a mystery, because the general sequence of events could have been reconstructed in any event; but a puzzle in which some major pieces are missing.

As it is, Pliny of course lived to write his letters, whose literary value

lies in their plasticity and in a style enlivened by the occasional use of
the historical present, which seasons the narrative with a touch of
immediacy. More important, however, is their truthfulness. The
author writes, for example, that the earthquake continued throughout
the eruption, which might incline the geologists among us to shake their
heads because such tremors tend to precede rather than accompany
eruptions . . . if some columns and statues had not been found to have
fallen on top of an already settled layer of lapilli, in other words, to
have toppled over long after the precipitation of volcanic wastes had
begun. Similarly the 'long fantastic flames'—*longae flammarum figurae*—
mentioned in the second letter might be taken for a fear-induced
hallucination if it had not since been discovered that large-scale
electrical discharges are a fairly frequent feature of steam-and-ash
eruptions. As early as 1879, the mineralogist Arcangelo Scacchi had
detected, in the ruins of Pompeii, no fewer than five localities which
had unquestionably been struck by lightning during the disaster.

There are other and subtler reasons as well for assessing highly the
reliability of this report, which represents the classic document, as it
were, of all vulcanology (geologists still call a certain type of eruption,
characterized by the formation of a cloud in the shape of a parasol pine,
a 'Plinian' eruption). It is true that Pliny wrote most of his letters in
the expectation of seeing them published, and therefore tends to reveal
less of himself than his model Cicero did in *his* correspondence. And it
is equally true that he occasionally exhibits a quite extraordinary
vanity, and that on being appointed to the senate in A.D. 100, he
delivered before that no longer august body an address of homage and
gratitude to Trajan which fairly drips with adulation; Macaulay wrote
that 'no University Sermon was ever more stupid' than this *panegyricus*.
Be that as it may, in his letters to Tacitus the author emerges as a
modest and highly trustworthy young man. A person who is urged, as
Pliny was by his uncle, to examine at close quarters an erupting
volcano, and who refuses because he wants to finish his homework
first, is not an ideal observer of such a phenomenon. Nonetheless, one
cannot read his account without a certain respect for its author. Writing
as he did at a time when few if any literate survivors of the catastrophe
can have been about, he may well have been tempted to embellish if

not his own actions, then at least the end which his uncle, Pliny the Elder, Admiral of the Roman Fleet and author of the *Natural History*, found in the doomed city; especially as he greatly admired the older man, whose property and name, Caius Plinius Caecilius Secundus, he was to inherit. It is to Pliny's credit that he did nothing of the sort, and that when his own behaviour *was* heroic or at least stoic, during the panic described in the second letter, he modestly disparages his own steadfastness with the remark that he, too, would have fled had he not believed that all mankind was being annihilated—*nisi me cum omnibus, omnia mecum perire . . . credidissem.*

The letters are concise and informative enough to be reproduced here, with minor omissions, in the suitably monumental Melmoth-Hutchinson translation.

'To Tacitus:

Your request that I would send you an account of my uncle's end, so that you may transmit a more exact relation of it to posterity, deserves my acknowledgements; for if his death shall be celebrated by your pen, the glory of it, I am aware, will be rendered for ever deathless . . .

He was at that time with the fleet under his command at Misenum. On the 24th of August, about one in the afternoon, my mother desired him to observe a cloud of very unusual size and appearance. He had sunned himself, then taken a cold bath, and after a leisurely luncheon was engaged in the study. He immediately called for his shoes and went up an eminence from whence he might best view this very uncommon appearance. It was not at that distance discernible from what mountain this cloud issued, but it was found afterwards to be Vesuvius. I cannot give you a more exact description of its figure, than by resembling it to that of a pine tree, for it shot up a great height in the form of a trunk, which extended itself at the top into several branches; because I imagine, a momentary gust of air blew it aloft, and then falling, forsook it; thus causing the cloud to expand laterally as it dissolved, or possibly the downward pressure of its own weight produced this effect. It was at one moment white, at another dark and spotted, as if it had carried up earth or cinders.

My uncle, true savant that he was, deemed the phenomenon

important and worth a nearer view. He ordered a light vessel to be got ready, and gave me the liberty, if I thought proper, to attend him. I replied I would rather study; and, as it happened, he had himself given me a theme for composition. As he was coming out of the house he received a note from Rectina, the wife of Bassus, who was in the utmost alarm at the imminent danger (his villa stood just below us, and there was no way to escape but by sea); she earnestly entreated him to save her from such deadly peril. He changed his first design and what he began with a philosophical, he pursued with an heroical turn of mind. He ordered large galleys to be launched and went himself on board one, with the intention of assisting not only Rectina, but many others; for the villas stand extremely thick upon that beautiful coast. Hastening to the place from whence others were flying, he steered his direct course to the point of danger and with such freedom from fear, as to be able to make and dictate his observations upon the successive motions and figures of that terrific object.

And now cinders, which grew thicker and hotter the nearer he approached, fell into the ships, then pumice-stones too, with stones blackened, scorched, and cracked by fire, then the sea ebbed suddenly from under them, while the shore was blocked up by land-slips from the mountains. After considering a moment whether he should retreat, he said to the captain who was urging that course 'Fortune befriends the brave; carry me to Pomponianus'. Pomponianus was then at Stabiae, distant by half the width of the bay (for, as you know, the shore, insensibly curving in its sweep, forms here a receptacle for the sea). He had already embarked his baggage for though at Stabiae the danger was not yet near, it was full in view and certain to be extremely near, as soon as it spread; and he resolved to fly as soon as the contrary wind should cease. It was full favourable, however, for carrying my uncle to Pomponianus. He embraces comforts, and encourages his alarmed friend, and in order to soothe the other's fears by his own unconcern, desires to be conducted to a bathroom; and after having bathed, he sat down to supper with great cheerfulness, or at least (what is equally heroic) with all the appearance of it.

In the meanwhile Mount Vesuvius was blazing in several places with spreading and towering flames, whose refulgent brightness the darkness of the night set in high relief. But my uncle, in order to soothe apprehensions, kept saying that some fires had been left alight by the terrified country people, and what they saw were only deserted villas on fire in the abandoned district. After this he retired to rest, and it is most certain that his rest was a most genuine slumber; for his breathing, which, as he was pretty fat, was somewhat heavy and sonorous, was heard by those who attended at his chamber-door. But the court which led to his apartment now lay so deep under a mixture of pumice-stones and ashes, that if he had continued longer in his bedroom, egress would have been impossible. On being aroused, he came out, and returned to Pomponianus and the others, who had sat up all night. They consulted together as to whether they should hold out in the house, or wander about in the open. For the house now tottered under repeated and violent concussions, and seemed to rock to and fro as if torn from its foundations. In the open air, on the other hand, they dreaded the falling pumice-stones, light and porous though they were; yet this, by comparison, seemed the lesser danger of the two; a conclusion which my uncle arrived at by balancing reasons, and the others by balancing fears. They tied pillows upon their heads with napkins; and this was their whole defence against the showers that fell round them.

It was now day everywhere else, but there a deeper darkness prevailed than in the most obscure night; relieved, however, by many torches and divers illuminations. They thought it proper to go down upon the shore to observe from close at hand if they could possibly put out to sea, but they found the waves still ran extremely high and contrary. There my uncle having thrown himself down upon a disused sail, repeatedly called for, and drank, a draught of cold water; soon after, flames, and a strong smell of sulphur, which was the forerunner of them, dispersed the rest of the company in flight; him they only aroused. He raised himself up with the assistance of two of his slaves, but instantly fell; some unusually gross vapour, as I conjecture, having obstructed his breathing and blocked his windpipe, which was not only naturally weak and constricted, but chronically inflamed. When day dawned again (the third from that he last beheld) his body was found entire and uninjured, and still fully clothed as in life; its posture was that of a sleeping, rather than a dead man.

Meanwhile my mother and I were at Misenum. But this has no connection with history, and your inquiry went no further than concerning my uncle's death. I will therefore put an end to my letter. Suffer me only to add, that I have faithfully related to you what I was either an eye-witness of myself, or heard at the time, when report speaks most truly. You will select what is most suitable to your purpose; for there is a great difference between a letter, and an history; between writing to a friend, and writing for the public. Farewell.'

* * *

'To Tacitus:

The letter which, in compliance with your request, I wrote to you concerning the death of my uncle, has raised, you say, your curiosity to know not only what terrors, but what calamities I endured when left behind at Misenum (for there I broke off my narrative).

"Though my shock'd soul recoils, my tongue shall tell!"[7]

My uncle having set out, I gave the rest of the day to study—the object which had kept me at home. After which I bathed, dined, and retired to short and broken slumbers. There had been for several days before some shocks of earthquake, which the less alarmed us as they are frequent in Campania; but that night they became so violent that one might think that the world was not merely shaken, but turned topsy-turvy. My mother flew to my chamber; I was just rising, meaning on my part to awaken her, if she was asleep. We sat down in the forecourt of the house, which separated it by a short space from the sea. I know not whether I should call it courage or inexperience—I was not quite eighteen—but I called for a volume of Livy, and began to read, and even went on with the extracts I was making from it, as if nothing were the matter. Lo and behold, a friend of my uncle's, who was just come to him from Spain, appears on the scene; observing my mother and me seated, and that I have

View of Vesuvius from the west showing it before the
eruption of AD 79. Bacchus and the serpent are on either
side of the volcano in this fresco found in Pompeii. Museo
Nazionale, Naples.

2a *Above* Johann Joachim Winckelmann. An engraving by
J.F. Bause after A. Maron. Staatliche Kunstsammlungen,
Weimar.

2b *Right* Bust of the Roman banker, moneychanger and
auctioneer Lucius Caecilius Jucundus. Museo Nazionale,
Naples.

actually a book in my hand, he sharply censures her patience and my indifference; nevertheless I still went on intently with my author.

It was now six o'clock in the morning, the light still ambiguous and faint. The buildings around us already tottered, and though we stood upon open ground, yet as the place was narrow and confined, there was certain and formidable danger from their collapsing. It was not till then we resolved to quit the town. The common people follow us in the utmost consternation, preferring the judgement of others to their own (wherein the extreme of fear resembles prudence), and impel us onwards by pressing in a crowd upon our rear. Being got outside the houses, we halt in the midst of a most strange and dreadful scene. The coaches which we had ordered out, though upon the most level ground, were sliding to and fro, and could not be kept steady even when stones were put against the wheels. Then we beheld the sea sucked back, and as it were repulsed by the convulsive motion of the earth; it is certain at least the shore was considerably enlarged, and now held many sea animals captive on the dry sand. On the other side, a black and dreadful cloud bursting out in gusts of igneous serpentine vapour now and again yawned open to reveal long fantastic flames, resembling flashes of lightning but much larger.

Our Spanish friend already mentioned now spoke with more warmth and instancy: "If your brother—if your uncle," said he, "is yet alive, he wishes you both may be saved; if he has perished, it was his desire that you might survive him. Why therefore do you delay your escape?" We could never think of our own safety, we said, while we were uncertain of his. Without more ado our friend hurried off, and took himself out of danger at the top of his speed.

Soon afterwards, the cloud I have described began to descend upon the earth, and cover the sea. It had already begirt the hidden Capreae [Capri], and blotted from sight the promontory of Misenum. My mother now began to beseech, exhort, and command me to escape as best I might; a young man could do it; she, burdened with age and corpulency, would die easy if only she had not caused my death. I replied, I would not be saved without her, and taking her by the hand, I hurried her on. She complies reluctantly and not without

3

reproaching herself for retarding me. Ashes now fall upon us, though as yet in no great quantity. I looked behind me; gross darkness pressed upon our rear, and came rolling over the land after us like a torrent. I proposed while we yet could see, to turn aside, lest we should be knocked down in the road by the crowd that followed us and trampled to death in the dark. We had scarce sat down, when darkness overspread us, not like that of a moonless or cloudy night, but of a room when it is shut up, and the lamp put out. You could hear the shrieks of women, the crying of children, and the shouts of men; some were seeking their children, others their parents, others their wives or husbands, and only distinguishing them by their voices; one lamenting his own fate, another that of his family; some praying to die, from the very fear of dying; many lifting their hands to the gods; but the greater part imagining that there were no gods left anywhere, and that the last and eternal night was come upon the world.

There were even some who augmented the real perils by imaginary terrors. Newcomers reported that such or such a building at Misenum had collapsed or taken fire—falsely, but they were credited. By degrees it grew lighter; which we imagined to be rather the warning of approaching fire (as in truth it was) than the return of day: however, the fire stayed at a distance from us: then again came darkness, and a heavy shower of ashes; we were obliged every now and then to rise and shake them off, otherwise we would have been buried and even crushed under their weight. I might have boasted that amidst dangers so appalling, not a sigh or expression of fear escaped from me, had not my support been founded in miserable, though strong consolation, that all mankind were involved in the same calamity, and that I was perishing with the world itself.

At last this dreadful darkness was attenuated by degrees to a kind of cloud or smoke, and passed away; presently the real day returned, and even the sun appeared, though lurid as when an eclipse is in progress. Every object that presented itself to our yet affrighted gaze was changed, cover'd over with a drift of ashes, as with snow. We returned to Misenum, where we refreshed ourselves as well as we could, and passed an anxious night between hope and fear; though indeed with a much larger share of the latter, for the earthquake still continued, and several enthusiastic people were giving a grotesque turn to their own and their neighbours' calamities by terrible predictions. Even then, however, my mother and I, notwithstanding the danger we had passed, and that which still threatened us, had no thoughts of leaving the place, till we should receive some tidings of my uncle.

And now, you will read this narrative, so far beneath the dignity of a history, without any view of transferring it to your own; and indeed you must impute it to your own request, if it shall appear scarce worthy of a letter. Farewell.'

In order to do full justice to the author's sang-froid and his refusal to garnish it with heroic or moralistic posturings, we must realize that he possessed no personal experience or scientific knowledge to fall back upon. For all that he could tell, the world *was* coming to an end. He did not understand, as the modern observer would, that what he had witnessed was a very dangerous but also a very localized upheaval of nature. His was not a generation inured, as ours is, to sudden shifts in the limits of Man's knowledge of the universe, to those scientific advances which we call 'break-throughs' precisely because they breach the wall in which the human mind had until then been encased. Our concepts of the physical universe are in flux; we are not shocked by the idea that mass may be considered as potential energy, or disheartened by the experience of seeing dismissed, as insufficient and no longer applicable, many working hypotheses which as recently as fifty years ago had been considered incontrovertible natural laws. The ancients, on the other hand, looked upon the universe as something firm, immutable except by direct divine intervention, and centred on the earth. It has been said that the stalwart Romans would have trembled had they known that the solid crust of the earth, on which they strode so proudly, is thinner, compared to the planet's liquid interior, than the skin of an apple is in relation to the whole fruit. To a man like Pliny, the eruption of Vesuvius must have been as staggering as the idea of a collision between moon and earth is to us. Yet it did not make him lose his composure or his sense of the *nil admirari*. He would die, if he must; but he would not waste on the prospect of death any fear, regret, or even curiosity. At the same time, he makes it plain that his uncle, who commanded a ship to be made ready so that he might go to Pompeii in order to bring help and to investigate the disaster on the spot, was a man of quite different calibre. But not even family pride could bring him to embroider fact with fiction. Suetonius, for example, writes in his biography of the Elder Pliny that according to some reports the admiral, finding himself near the burning city with all escape cut off, had himself run through by a slave. This of course was the Roman gentleman's way of dying under such circumstances, and if it had been his uncle's, Pliny would surely have mentioned it approvingly. The admiral, however, was an obese and asthmatic man of fifty-six, and we may assume that his end, while gallantly met, was in no way inspiring: overcome by smoke, and weakened by the shortness of breath resulting from what the text delicately calls '*amplitudo corporis*,' he simply lay down and died. In the past two centuries, the remains of several Pompeiians have been found who had been holding pieces of cloth to their faces, in an attempt to escape death by asphyxiation. They, too, gave the impression of 'sleeping, rather than . . . dead' people.[8]

External and internal evidence thus bears out the truthfulness of Pliny's description. Many of the salient features of the eruption can be deduced from it, but the picture is necessarily incomplete because the author was so far removed from the event in time and space. In the intervening years, he must have forgotten much of what he had lived through as a very young man. And even if he had been adventurous rather than lethargic, and accompanied his uncle to Pompeii instead of reading his Livy at home, he would still have arrived on the scene at a relatively late date: towards evening of the first day. By the time the admiral's barge landed, most of the inhabitants who had remained behind must have died, slain by collapsing buildings or asphyxiated by mephitic gases. Only those who were trapped and eventually died of starvation (like the woman found in the House of the Vestals, whose body had been gnawed by her dog before the animal died in its turn) can possibly have been left alive by then. But the great majority had fled in any case, and it was probably not only unwise but impossible to approach the city that evening on either a humanitarian or a reportorial errand. The distance which separated Pliny from the scene accounts for some other insufficiencies in his description. Thus it is odd that he should make no mention of the tremendous detonation which must have preceded the eruption. His friend Valerius Flaccus refers to the bellowing of the splitting mountain.[9] Dio Cassius claims to have heard the eruption of A.D. 202 from as far away as Capua, and in the eighteenth century, De Brosses wrote that whenever Vesuvius is about to erupt, there issues from it 'a noise reminiscent of thunder';[10] the terrifying detonation of Mont Pelé and the Soufrière in this century has likewise been remarked upon by every eye- or earwitness. Another disputed point arises not from an omission on Pliny's part but from the textual history of the letters. In an early codex, the date is given as *Nonum Kal. Septembres*, i.e., *ante dies nonum Kalendas Septembres*, or August 24. Other and later codices, including the *editio princeps* of 1471, read *Non. Kal. Decembres*, or November 23 (the irrepressible Mark Twain for some reason gives November 9 as the date in *The Innocents Abroad*). The majority of experts favour the earlier date, basing their argument among other things on the empty wine vats found in Pompeii and nearby Boscoreale, which seem to indicate that the end came before the grape harvest had been gathered. But there is enough ammunition available to the other side, such as the discovery of late-ripening fruit which had just been picked and of a number of bodies in winter clothing, to have kept up a lively if sporadic scholarly skirmish on this question, which can now be considered to have been settled in favour of August 24.

The importance of Pliny's letters should not blind us to the fact that most of the references to Pompeii found in ancient literature antedate the city's destruction. Mention has already been made of Strabo, Vitruvius, and others who describe at least the general region in which Pompeii is located; these references from the period before A.D. 79, however, are too brief and incidental to be of much interest. With the exception of Pliny, the later authors, writing about a city no longer extant, tend to do so in a moralizing fashion, as Statius does in the *epicedium* or dirge on his father's death[11] and Martial in his famous epigram.

In view of the magnitude of the disaster, the lack of any contemporary literary response is astounding. It may be that the extent and suddenness of the calamity paralyzed a poetic imagination whose heroic vein had in any case long become exhausted. After depicting so many legendary upheavals, the writers of the period appear to have been struck speechless by the very real catastrophe which had taken place in their own lifetime. Thus it is not altogether surprising that the most rewarding contemporary evidence should lie buried in a minor and almost subterranean form of literature, in the so-called Sibylline Books, or collections of oracular wisdom supposedly dispensed by the various sibyls (whose number Varro gave as ten). In reality, these were warnings, exhortations, and other comments anonymously composed by men who described contemporary events under the *nom de plume*, as it were, of a sibyl prophesying the future. (These Sibylline Books thus differ from the official *Libri Sibyllini*, consulted in times of national crisis as sacred documents containing prophecies relating to the future of the Roman Republic and Empire.) In an attempt to demonstrate the reliability of the unofficial or 'counterfeit' prophecies, Plutarch has someone say in an imaginary conversation:

'And these recent and unusual occurrences near Cumae and Dicearcheia, were they not recited long ago in the songs of the Sibyl? And has not Time, as if in her debt, duly discharged the obligation in the bursting forth of fires from the mountain, boiling seas, blazing rocks tossed aloft by the wind, and the destruction of such great and noble cities that those who came here by daylight felt ignorance and uncertainty as to where these had been situated, since the land was in such confusion?'[12]

This listing of the disaster among the calamities foretold by the Sibyl is underlined by a passage in the Fourth Sibylline Book, which reads like the description of a past event rather than the prophecy which it purports to be:

'When the fire escaping from the broken earth of Italy reaches the open sky, it will burn many cities and kill many men; the wide sky will be full of ashes while drops like ochre fall. Recognize then the wrath of gods [God?] in heaven, because they will destroy the innocent tribe of the pious.'

These lines may have been written in the year A.D. 79, because there is no mention, in this book which is essentially a catalogue of woes about to befall mankind, of the great fire which devastated Rome the following year. It is not surprising that the destruction of Herculaneum and Pompeii should have been considered as an act of divine retribution against those who would persecute the 'tribe of the pious', εὐσεβέων γῦλονι after all, the Sibylline Books were largely composed by Hellenized Jews, and the Great Eruption took place in the reign of the same Titus who had just levelled the Temple in Jerusalem. Tertullian and others who later reflected on the fate of the Campanian cities were reminded of Sodom and Gomorrha; but much earlier, an unknown Jew or Christian had already scratched the words SODOMA GOMORA on the wall of the *triclinium* of a Pompeiian house. Although it is tempting to think that this graffito might date from August 24, A.D. 79, and represent what would surely be the briefest and most scathing 'eye-witness report' recorded by history, the available evidence indicates that it was made many years later, possibly by a former resident who dug his way through the cooled-off ashes in order to save what he could of his belongings, or steal what he could carry away of someone else's.[13]

These conjectures touch on two important questions which are still waiting to be fully resolved: how deeply had the ancients penetrated, in the years following the disaster, into the buried city before the site was finally abandoned? And to what extent, if any, had Christianity taken root among those who died, or escaped, in A.D. 79? The implications of the first question are archaeological, revolving around the possibility that a portion of this city, which has had to be laboriously rediscovered ever since the mid-eighteenth century, was actually being re-rediscovered. The implications of the second question are in part literary, revolving around the possibility that those set-pieces of fiction localized in Pompeii, the Christian Maiden ravished by heathen lust or thrown to the lions and the Christian Youth shaken in his new-found faith by the wiles of a pagan temptress, are perhaps not so fictional after all. The intricate nature of both problems, and the ingenuity which has been applied to resolving them at least in part, are best illustrated by taking a brief detour through the varied interpretations given of the famous magic square, which has been found in the following two forms:

```
ROTAS          SATOR
OPERA          AREPO
TENET          TENET
AREPO          OPERA
SATOR   and    ROTAS
```

Each column can be read vertically as well as horizontally, and a perfect palindrome results even if the words are written out in a line: ROTAS OPERA TENET AREPO SATOR—SATOR AREPO TENET OPERA ROTAS. At one time, this cryptogram was thought to be medieval in origin; representing, possibly, the five nails which held Christ to the cross, it appears to have been used as an amulet for propitiatory and other magic purposes: to protect against fire, to call for help in childbirth, to ward off or cure disease. It is recorded that in sixteenth-century Lyons, a patient was healed on being given pieces of bread to eat, each of which was inscribed with a portion of the magic square. The emblem has been found in buildings and in liturgical formulae of the Coptic Church of Ethiopia, on houses in France, in churches in Asia Minor, and in a Carolingian Bible dating back to A.D. 822. In 1868, however, the presumed date of its origin had to be advanced to antiquity; that year, an example of it was discovered in Cirencester, England, in Roman ruins of the third century A.D.

For a long time, the word *arepo*, non-existent in Latin, vitiated all attempts at a feasible interpretation of the text encapsulated in this emblem. It is now considered by some to have been derived from a Celtic term for 'plow', as found in the Latinized *arepennis:* area plowed in one day, or at any one time, by a team of oxen. In that case, a rough translation (depending on the sequence in which the five words are arranged) might mean anything from 'The sower with his plow carefully guides the wheels' to the 'God is the creator and keeper of all things' which some particularly imaginative scholars have professed to see in it. If the emblem was used as password, greeting, or other sign of recognition by crypto-Christians who had reason to arouse no suspicions on the part of their pagan fellow-citizens, its 'message' could be rendered obvious by simply throwing into relief the centre lines,

```
r o Ta s        s a To r
o p Er a        a r Ep o
TE NE T         TE NE T
a r Ep o        o p Er a
s a To r        r o Ta s,
```

in which case it would form a Greek cross.

Dissatisfied with this solution which he considered only partial, a German clergyman, Felix Grosser of Chemnitz, proceeded in 1926 to rearrange the letters. Concluding that the N, which aside from occupying the centre position of each square is also the only letter to occur but once, must remain the hinge on which the entire cryptogram turns, he arrived at the following layout:

```
              A
              ‾
              P
              A
              T
              E
              R
A/PATERNOSTER/O
              O
              S
              T
              E
              R
              ‾
              O
```

This arrangement is three-dimensional in that it represents the shape of the crucifix, the beginning of the Lord's Prayer in Latin, and the Biblical *alpha* and *omega* (Latin A and O). The third of these meanings, furthermore, is embodied even in the square itself, in which the letter T—Greek *tau*, a frequent crypto-Christian symbol because of its cross-like shape (although some experts insist that the cross did not acquire this symbolic extension until long after the first century)—at the beginning and end of *tenet* is flanked, vertically as well as horizontally, by an A and O:

```
r OTAs          s ATOr
Oper A          Ar ep O
Tene T          Tene T
Ar ep O         Oper A
s ATOr          r OTAs
```

In the years following Grosser's reconstruction, other examples of the magic square were discovered in Mesopotamia and elsewhere. Going back to late Roman times, they were contemporary with the one which had been found in Cirencester, and the palindrome's origin thus seemed to have been explained as satisfactorily as its meaning. This, however, had no sooner been achieved than the whole edifice threatened to collapse under the impact of a new development: on November 12, 1936, Matteo Della Corte found a copy of the magic square inscribed on a column of the *palaestra* adjoining the Pompeiian amphitheatre, which in turn enabled him to decipher another square, discovered somewhat earlier in truncated form in the House of P. Paquius Proculus.[14] With this, and the additional discovery, made in February 1939 in the House of the Bicentenary at Herculaneum, of what seemed to have been a Christian sanctuary complete with a wooden *prie-Dieu* and the shape of a crucifix impressed on a stuccoed wall, the interpretation of the square became once again a matter of dispute. For how could an emblem by which persecuted Christians supposedly communicated with one another and invoked divine aid in their tribulations, have been used in Pompeii if:

(*a*) it is unlikely, despite St Paul's landing at Pozzuoli which is described in the *Acts of the Apostles*, that there were enough Christians in Campania to require a sanctuary previous to A.D. 79, let alone to the earthquake of A.D. 63, which the Pompeiian square antedated?

(*b*) the early Christians prayed in Greek, and thus presumably had little use for an emblem which carries a full meaning only in Latin?

(*c*) the Greek *tau* as well as *alpha* and *omega*, represented by Latin T, A, and O, were not charged with any symbolic meaning until the *Epistle of Barnabas* and the *Apocalypse of John*, i.e., the period A.D. 75–90? And if the square had not been used by Christians after all, despite the seemingly faultless solution provided by Grosser, by whom and for what purpose *had* it been used, not only in Pompeii but throughout the extent of the Roman Empire?

Some now see in it a pagan emblem in which the 'sower' represents Mithras, and the wheels which he guides those of the solar chariot; others take it to be a Gnostic symbol, or a Judaic one based on a vision of Ezekiel, according to which the wheels would be those of the chariot carrying the wrath of God. More convincing than either of these hypotheses is a third one, namely, that the square's presence in Pompeii can be explained by the fact that in the decades following the eruption of A.D. 79, some more or less clandestine excavations were undertaken by men who were, to all intents and purposes, grave robbers: robbers of the mass grave which the entombed city had become. There is evidence that much of what has been brought to light in Pompeii had indeed been sifted first by these amateur explorers of long ago. For example, the inscription ΔΟΥΜΜΟC ΠΕΡΤΟΥCΑ *domus pertusa* ('house broken into') which Fiorelli discovered in the 1860s in the House of the Popidii Prisci, suggests that someone other than the owner had entered this building after its destruction; if the visitor had been the master of the house, he would presumably not have left behind a valuable statue which he could have salvaged as easily as the archaeologists salvaged it eighteen hundred years later. Also, the graffito found by Della Corte in the House of the Golden Cupids,[15] *quinquaginta ubi erant adsunt exinde iacentes*, may well have been a message left by a band of robbers, warning those who came after them of the presence of many skeletons—'there were fifty of them, still lying where they had been'.

According to this hypothesis, then, the magic square is indeed Christian in origin and carries the meaning suggested by Grosser. It dates from around A.D. 180, when Latin had begun to replace Greek as the liturgical language of the Christian Church, and its geographical point of origin is probably the region around Lugdunum or Lyons, where the term *arepo* was in common usage and where a local tradition had kept the cryptogram alive until the sixteenth century. The square's occurrence in Pompeii, like that of SODOMA GOMORA, must in that case be due to Christians who, finding themselves overtaken by fear, remorse, compassion, or some other emotion which they wished to communicate to others, perpetuated the record of their explorations within the subterranean city. This interpretation is the more compelling as it has since been determined, from the examination of a different body of evidence, that the supposed sanctuary in Herculaneum had probably not been used by Christians after all (a vital link in this chain of reasoning because Herculaneum, unlike Pompeii, had been overwhelmed not by a relatively light layer of ashes, lapilli, and earth, but by a mud avalanche which, hardening and becoming almost impenetrable, admitted of no amateurish tunnelling). As matters stand now, it is considered unlikely that definite proof of a Christian presence in Pompeii will ever be brought forth; if such a presence can be postulated at all, it must have been negligible in numbers and importance.

We must now turn to the last major ancient writer who left an account of the destruction of Pompeii and Herculaneum: Dio Cassius, author of a 'Roman History' in eighty volumes of which about a third has been preserved. Dealing with events from Aeneas' landing down to the author's own consulship in A.D. 229, the work represents one of the encyclopedic compilations of fact and fancy of which the ancients were so fond. For some reason, possibly because it was written in Greek, the Byzantines looked upon Dio's work as a major historical source, and Book 66, part of which is here cited in H.B. Foster's translation, owes its survival to the fact that an emperor of the eleventh century had the monk Xiphilinus prepare an abridged version. After a general description which reads as if based on personal observation, Dio has this to say about the eruption:

'Such is Vesuvius, and these phenomena usually occur there every year. But all the other occurrences that had taken place there in the course of time, however notable, because unusual, they may have seemed to those who on each occasion observed them, nevertheless would be regarded as trivial in comparison with what now happened, even if it all had been combined into one. This was what befell. Numbers of huge men quite surpassing any human stature—such creatures, in fact, as the giants are pictured to have been—appeared, now on the mountain, now in the surrounding country, and again in the cities, wandering over the earth day and night and also flitting through the air. After this fearful droughts and sudden and violent earthquakes occurred, so that the whole plain round about seethed and the summits leaped into the air. There were frequent rumblings, some of them subterranean, that resembled thunder, and some on the surface, that sounded like bellowings; the sea also joined in the roar and the sky re-echoed it. Then suddenly a portentous crash was heard, as if the mountains were tumbling in ruins; and first huge stones were hurled aloft, rising as high as the very summits, then came a great quantity of fire and endless smoke, so that the whole atmosphere was obscured and the sun was entirely hidden, as if eclipsed. Thus day was turned into night and light into darkness. Some thought that the giants were rising again in revolt (for at this time also many of their forms could be discerned in the smoke and, moreover, a sound as of trumpets was heard), while others believed that the whole universe was being resolved into chaos or fire. Therefore they fled, some from the houses into the streets, others from outside into the houses, now from the sea to the land and now from the land to the sea; for in their excitement they regarded any place where they were not as safer than where they were. While this was going on, an inconceivable quantity of ashes was blown out, which covered both sea and land and filled all the air. It wrought much injury of various kinds, as chance befell, to men and farms and cattle, and in particular it destroyed all fish and birds. Furthermore, it buried two entire cities, Herculaneum and Pompeii, the latter place while its populace was seated in the theatre. Indeed, the amount of dust, taken all together, was so great that some of it reached Africa and Syria and Egypt, and it also reached Rome, filling the air overhead and darkening the sun. There, too, no little fear was occasioned, that lasted for several days, since the people did not know and could not imagine what had happened, but, like those close at hand, believed that the whole world was being turned upside down, that the sun was disappearing into the earth and that the earth was being lifted to the sky. These ashes, now, did the Romans no great harm at the time, though later they brought a terrible pestilence upon them.'

Dio Cassius was born about a century after the eruption, and his account understandably lacks the personal involvement of Pliny's. We do not even know the sources on which he drew for this chapter; it has been surmised that they were the same that Suetonius used for his biography of the Elder Pliny. But even if based on secondary sources, Dio's description corresponds rather closely to Pliny's: we hear of the same earthquake especially at the beginning, the discharge of rocks, complete darkness at midday, and a great precipitation of volcanic wastes. Nor is there any reason to question certain additions of Dio's, such as the 'portentous crash' which signalled the splitting open of the crater, or the precipitation of ashes in localities far removed from the mountain. Both are standard by-products of major eruptions of this type. Some other modifications, however, are less credible. It is, for example, very unlikely that the inhabitants of Pompeii should have assembled in the amphitheatre at noon on August 24. The notion that the populace might thus have gathered—by divine disposition, as it were—in order to meet their doom collectively, is dramatically effective, which is no doubt why Bulwer used it in his story. But no bodies have been found on that site, and from what is known of Pompeiian history, it is highly improbable that any games were held there at all after the disturbances of A.D. 59, when civil strife had broken out after the gladiatorial combats.

Equally improbable, although mentioned also by Suetonius and Eusebius, is the derivation of the pestilence from the ashes emitted by Mount Vesuvius. There was a plague in Titus' reign, to be sure, one of the epidemics which recurred, with melancholy regularity, throughout ancient and medieval times; but its genesis is surely not to be found in the volcano. A more indicative detail may be seen in the mention of Pompeii and Herculaneum by name, a feature lacking in Pliny's account. Had the very memory of the cities so far receded that it had to be specifically revived for readers in the third century? The remaining details with which Dio adorns his story, are little more than fantasy. He merely gives rein to the penchant for the supernatural which characterizes his entire work, and as one compares these two accounts of the same event, written by authors who lived little more than a century apart, one comes away with a chilling realization of that clouding of Man's vision of the universe which was both a cause and a result of the decadence of ancient civilization. The contrast is striking indeed. Like most of his contemporaries, Pliny was so naïve in questions of natural science that he mistook a volcanic eruption for the end of the world. Nonetheless he preserved intact what little curiosity and initiative the gods had given him, along with a full measure of courage and consideration for the old and humble. Never, one feels, would this rational human being have fallen back on the half-forgotten legend of the Phlegraean Fields, and entertained the idea that gigantic bogeymen were rising forth from the mountain to the accompaniment of infernal trumpets.

When Dio wrote, this bedrock of reason and self-reliance had become eroded. Signs and portents had replaced observation and deduction, and we suddenly find ourselves closer to the Middle Ages than to the Augustan Age. The literary tradition of Pompeii in ancient times thus closes on the same note of eeriness and wonderment on which it began. The wheel had come full circle and Vesuvius was once more, as it had been a thousand years before, the abode of giants trying to escape from under its weight.

2

The Rediscovery: Classicism and Absolutism

'One hates writing descriptions that are to be found in every book of travels; but we have seen something today that I am sure you never read of, and perhaps never heard of. Have you ever heard of a subterraneous town? A whole Roman town, with all its edifices, remaining under ground?'

Horace Walpole to Richard West, 14 June 1740

FROM THE FALL of the Roman Empire to the beginning of modern times, the forgotten cities slumbered undisturbed in the ground—Pompeii under vineyards gradually taken into cultivation on top of the ashes, Herculaneum forty to sixty feet below the petrified mud on which the city of Resina had meanwhile risen. In the course of these centuries, southern Italy was ruled at various times by the Germanic tribes, the Byzantines, the Normans, the Hohenstaufen emperors of Germany, the Angevin kings of France, and the Aragonese kings of Spain. During the Renaissance, when the ancient world became a subject of study and its literature and art an object of emulation, the memory of Pompeii and Herculaneum was occasionally revived; not with a view to finding, let alone excavating them, but because they had been mentioned by writers whose works were now being closely examined. Nourished by the author's reading, a reference to Pompeii is thus found in Boccaccio's *L'Ameto*, and the vision of an undamaged city whose buildings could be seen *quasi integri* in the twelfth chapter of Sannazaro's *Arcadia* (1502). Yet even the Renaissance passed its zenith without any attempt being made to find the precise spot where Pompeii had been, although the name given to the general area, *civitas* or *città*, seemed to embody a distant recollection, preserved down the ages, of a city that had once lain there. In order to safeguard the water supply of Torre d'Annunziata and other coastal towns, canals were dug in the region and remnants of buildings brought to light; but hardly anyone thought of connecting these chance discoveries with the legend

3 Papyrus from Herculaneum which is part of Philodemus' *Treatise on Music*, one of the first works to be unrolled without disintegrating.

4a *Above* Villa of Julia Felix showing the garden and pools and, on the right, the peristyle with its fluted pilasters.

4b *Below* The amphitheatre at Pompeii: a general view of the cavea and part of the tiers.

of the lost cities. In retrospect, it seems strange that men of much talent and imagination—such as Sannazaro himself, or the architect and engineer Domenico Fontana who erected the obelisk in front of St Peter's in Rome and built the Palazzo Reale in Naples, or the German savant Holstenius who had actually asserted, in 1637, that Pompeii could be found under the hill of *civitas*—should have lived and worked in the area without testing these hypotheses by simply sinking a few exploratory shafts. However, it was not without reason that another century was to pass before digging began in earnest. The two towns are by no means the only ancient settlements which disappeared under the ashes of Vesuvius, and for every expert claiming to have found their actual location, another would step forward to dispute the claim, on evidence which in default of tangible proof appeared equally sound; Naples was a major apple of discord in the wars which Spain, France, and Austria waged for supremacy on the Italian peninsula, and few were the years in which the arts of peace were allowed to flourish unrestrained; the volcano guarded its victims jealously in erupting, in December 1631 and again a few years later, as violently as it had in 79. Even more important than these physical obstacles was a psychological one: there was simply no precedent for the restoration of a buried city. Archaeology as we know it had its cradle in Pompeii and Herculaneum, and all later excavations and restorations, whether undertaken in Greece or Mesopotamia or Peru or Egypt or elsewhere, are essentially variations on a theme first played in the shade of Mount Vesuvius. Under these circumstances, it is no wonder that the theme should have set in hesitantly, and so discordantly at first that it can be said to have begun in the wrong place, at the wrong time, and for the wrong reason.

What set it in motion was the chance discovery, in 1711, of some stone and masonry fragments which the peasant Giovanni Battista Nocerino of Resina had dug up while deepening a well. These fragments were brought to the attention of Emanuel Maurice of Lorraine, Prince d'Elboeuf, an Austrian cavalry officer attached to the Neapolitan court who was having a country house built on the beach of Granatello near Portici. Realizing that the material must have come from a Roman villa, he purchased the land on which it had been found and undertook some clandestine explorations of his own. Although he did not know it

4

at the time, he had hit upon the amphitheatre of Herculaneum from which he now extracted, along with many lesser objects, three female statues of rare perfection. They were excellent Roman reproductions of a Greek matron and two younger women. After repairing what damage they had suffered (ever since the Renaissance, whole sculptures, even if mediocre, had been esteemed higher than fragments of a masterpiece) he smuggled these so-called 'Vestal Virgins' out of Naples in order to present them to his commander-in-chief and distant cousin, the Austrian general Prince Eugene, who in turn exhibited them in his palace in Vienna. There the marble ladies excited all the admiration to which their beauty and the adventurous manner of their discovery entitled them, and when their owner died, Augustus III of Poland (Frederick Augustus II in his capacity as Elector of Saxony) bought them for the Dresden *Antikensaal*, which housed what was then, along with the Arundelian at Oxford, the finest collection of classical sculpture outside Italy.

D'Elboeuf having left Portici when the Austrians withdrew their forces from Naples, nothing was done to follow up his startling discovery until Charles III was proclaimed King of the Two Sicilies in 1734. This son of Philip V of Spain and Elisabeth Farnese was the first of the Neapolitan Bourbons who were to rule southern Italy, i.e., Sicily and the mainland to just below Terracina, until the country's unification in the last century. In 1738, he married Maria Amalia of Saxony, and the young queen, reared at the art-loving court of Dresden, had no sooner arrived in Naples than she saw to it that the work initiated by D'Elboeuf was continued. Charles III, who had already requisitioned the Austrian's property at Portici, with the disinterred art objects which had been stored in the basement of the villa, now ordered Roque Joaquín de Alcubierre, a Spanish engineering officer in his army, to explore the site of Herculaneum in a systematic fashion. Much of value was brought to light in the next few years, including, in April 1748, the first body of a victim of the Great Eruption; while often interrupted, the work has never been officially discontinued from that time to the present. No one could then have known that Pompeii, which was not discovered until ten and identified until fifteen years later, would have been a more rewarding spot in which to begin these endeavours. Bigger than Herculaneum and more important in classical times, it was to yield a far wider and more valuable range of objects; only lightly covered by ashes and lapilli instead of being encased in hardened mud (which had become almost impenetrable by the lava of 1631), it was more accessible; because of its location in relatively open country, its eventual exploration entailed none of the technical and legal problems connected with tunnelling under the foundations of an inhabited town such as Resina, where much of Herculaneum remains buried to this day.

The excavation of entire cities is a large-scale enterprise, which in the Age of Absolutism could only be carried out with the ruling prince's support. Inevitably, the personalities of Charles III and his successor Ferdinand IV have left their imprint on the resurrection of Pompeii and Herculaneum, and idle though it may be, one is tempted to wish that this resurrection had got underway not toward the middle but at the very beginning of Charles' reign, in which case it might have acquired sufficient momentum to carry it through the rule of his son. As things turned out, the work had barely begun when Charles and Maria Amalia were forced to relinquish Naples and to exchange the Sicilian crown for that of Spain—the Austrians having exacted, in return for agreeing to the installation of the Bourbons in Naples, a stipulation that the Kingdoms of the Two Sicilies and of Spain were never to be governed, in personal union, by one and the same monarch. On the death of his half-brother Ferdinand VI of Spain, in 1759, Charles accordingly transferred his court to Madrid and entrusted Naples and Sicily to his son, also named Ferdinand, who was then a boy of eight.

Although he cannot be compared to Frederick the Great or Maria Theresa, Charles III differed favourably from the Austrian viceroys who had preceded and the Bourbon kings who were to follow him; indeed, he stands almost alone among the later representatives of that dynasty as a not unworthy descendant of the Sun King. The foundation of the Neapolitan Academy of Art; the transfer, 'within the family' as it were, of the Farnese treasures from Parma to Naples; the relocation of the University of Naples in the Palazzo degli Studii—all these activities bear witness to the perspicacity and energy of this sovereign, especially if we take into account the relative briefness of his reign (twenty-five years, compared to Frederick the Great's forty-six and Louis XV's fifty-nine) and the sound political and economic position in which he left the Two Sicilies at the end of it. It was very well for De Brosses to quote Molière's '*Cet homme assurément n'aime pas la musique*' on observing that the king talked during one half of a performance and slept during the other. But it was Charles III who had had the theatre built, the famous San Carlo Opera (so named because it was inaugurated on his Saint's Day, on 4 November 1738), which perpetuates his memory the more deservedly as its construction was not a vain–glorious gesture but a fitting tribute to the Naples in which Metastasio, Scarlatti, and Pergolesi had lived and in which Porpora and Paisiello were to die. Of all the monarchs of Europe, only Charles III and the mad Ludwig of Bavaria extended themselves so generously on behalf of this particular Muse.

Charles III was an absolute monarch, and he acted like one; when leaving for Spain, he thought nothing of dismantling the porcelain manufacture of Capodimonte and reassembling it at Buen Retiro. But if he was autocratic, he also had the good sense to select his servants wisely. Beginning with Bernardo Tanucci, the law professor whom he imported from Tuscany and made Prime Minister, and the architect Vanvitelli who designed the palace and gardens of Caserta, more magnificent in some respects than those of Versailles itself, he appointed to high office men of competence and of unquestioned personal integrity, a trait which was so marked in himself that he punctiliously left behind in Naples, as state property, a ring that had been presented to him on the occasion of a visit to the excavations. In regard to these, his touch was less sure. As has been said, they represented a pioneering venture; Alcubierre showed himself competent enough as an engineer, but lacked all notion of art and even that elementary sense of piety toward the past which forms the basis of all archaeology. Ottavio Baiardi, placed in charge of identifying and cataloguing what Alcubierre had unearthed, was a political appointee who, instead of listing the finds, compiled a number of *prodromi* or introductory essays dealing not with Herculaneum, but with the legendary exploits of that Hercules who had been the town's supposed founder. The elaborate retelling of these fables created much discontent among the scholars of the day, who, understandably enough, were interested not so much in the Augean Stables as in the new discoveries which, as rumour had it, among other things outshone all examples of ancient painting that had hitherto been discovered. When these rumblings had become too loud to be disregarded, Baiardi was dismissed and the task of publishing the results of the excavations given to the fifteen members of the Academy of Herculaneum. This body of experts, established in 1755 along the lines of the Etruscan Academy of Cortona and other learned societies of the period, was to issue a series of volumes entitled *Antichità d'Ercolano*, the first of which appeared in 1757. These engravings of statues, coins, paintings and the like were instrumental in spreading to every corner of Europe the Pompeiian and Herculanean motifs which later found their way into neoclassical architecture, painting, and above all, interior decoration. Winckelmann, the Comte de Caylus, and many others criticized the Academy for the dilatoriness of its publications and for the many inaccuracies which these contained; yet the nine volumes of the *Antichità d'Ercolano* were splendidly bound and illustrated and could be issued only because Charles III had granted the printer a subsidy out of his privy purse.

All this was to change under Ferdinand IV, or Ferdinand I as he called himself after the Congress of Vienna. He reigned from 1759 to 1825, with the enthusiastic approval of the Neapolitan mob which fondly called him 'Nasone' on account of his bulbous nose and recognized in him one of their own: a *lazzarone* at heart and in manner who spoke dialect, sold in the public market, and at a stiff price, the fish he had caught in the bay, and was as skilful as the humblest of his subjects in warding off the Evil Eye. They misunderstood him only once, when he did a good deed in founding the silk factory of San Leucio near Caserta; convinced that this idealistic project was but a façade behind which the king was assembling his private harem, the Neapolitans took to calling the workers' children '*figli del Re*'. Neither Tanucci, who had been appointed regent until the prince came of age, nor Maria Carolina, the daughter of Maria Theresa (and sister of Joseph II and Marie Antoinette) who became his consort, nor his father who attempted to guide him by means of letters sent from far-away Madrid were able to ruffle Ferdinand's indolent bonhomie or to deflect him from his love of the hunt and his propensity for crude practical jokes, or to puncture his indifference to anything not directly related to his physical well-being. Sir William Hamilton, who became resident English minister in 1764 and thus had many opportunities to observe Ferdinand's development, has described the young husband as follows:

'On the morning after his nuptials, which took place in the beginning of May 1768, when the weather was very warm, he rose at an early hour and went out as usual to the chase, leaving his young wife in bed. Those courtiers who accompanied him, having inquired of his majesty how he liked her: *"Dorme come un'ammazzata,"* replied he, *"e suda come un porco"* [she sleeps as if she had been killed, and sweats like a pig]. Such an answer would be esteemed, anywhere except at Naples, most indecorous; but here we are familiarized to far greater violations of propriety and decency . . . When the King has made a hearty meal and feels an inclination to retire, he commonly communicates that intention to the noblemen around him in waiting, and selects the favoured individuals, whom, as a mark of predilection, he chooses shall attend him. *"Sono ben pranzato,"* says he, laying his hand on his belly, *"adesso bisogna una buona panciata"* [I have eaten well, now I need to move my bowels]. The persons thus preferred then accompany his majesty, stand respectfully round him, and amuse him by their conversation during the performance.'[1]

No sustained interest in the excavations could be expected of this man, and that none was forthcoming, beyond the brief thrill of novelty, is abundantly shown by the account which Joseph II of Austria left of his visit to Pompeii; it was on this occasion that Maria Carolina made the memorable comment that her husband, the King of the Two Sicilies, was 'a right good fool'—*ein recht guter Narr*.

How foolish Ferdinand was in regard to the excavations—which he nonetheless loved to show off to visitors as an attraction unique to his realm—is borne out by his order, given before his last visit to Pompeii in the 1820's, that the stepping-stones placed athwart the street, which had enabled the ancients to cross dry-footed while yet allowing chariot wheels to pass unhindered, be removed so that the low-slung royal carriage could drive through (they have since been replaced). Small wonder that the archaeologist who shortly afterwards guided the cultured Crown Prince of Bavaria, the later Ludwig I, through the ruins could not suppress the wistful remark that under a monarch of *that* kind, the city would have been laid free long ago! It was in Ferdinand's reign that three abuses which had begun in his father's day became general practice: the arbitrary restoration of one damaged object even if it meant pilfering another (which would provide, say, the missing arm of a statue); the removal of earth and ashes not away from the site altogether, but merely from one building to another which had been excavated, with the result that the total area cleared hardly increased at all; and the habit of considering the work site as nothing more than a source of supply for the royal museums. In a grotesque distortion of physiocratic reasoning, Ferdinand looked upon the archaeological treasure buried in the soil of his kingdom as so much potential dynastic wealth. Only the most valuable and best preserved finds were therefore taken to Portici and later, when Vesuvius threatened to engulf the region once again, to the Museo Borbonico (now Nazionale) in Naples. Everything else was smashed, left lying about, or carried off secretly like the two bronze candelabra which Goethe admired in Hamilton's house, where they had, as the poet tactfully put it, 'found their way' from the Pompeiian tombs.

Motivated as they were not by scholarly but by prestige and pecuniary factors, the excavations turned into a treasure hunt and as such had to be carried out in secret. The restrictions under which visitors laboured, and the suspiciousness with which they were regarded as potential thieves, form a recurrent theme in the reminiscences left by those who had had the good fortune of being admitted to these exclusive precincts in the first place. Any visitor, guide, or workman who possessed enough initiative and daring to break the royal monopoly on archaeological finds was able to do so by selling the stolen goods in the black market in *Pompeiiana* which eventually developed in Rome. Long after Ferdinand's death, in 1849, Friedrich Hebbel could still record that a Pompeiian guide had advised him: 'Take a good look around. If anything strikes your fancy, let me know. I shall steal it for you as soon as the moon is full.'[2]

A hint of these and similar abuses is found in the earliest literary reflection of the rediscovery of the Campanian cities, Charles de Brosses' *Lettres familières écrites d'Italie en 1739 et 1740*. Although his writings on the history of navigation, which once influenced mariners like Cook, Bougainville, and Vancouver, are as forgotten now as is his quarrel with Voltaire over a few cords of wood to which both men laid claim, De Brosses' travel journal still occupies an honoured place in literature. As the scion of an old Savoyard family, as a man of consequence in his own right who later became presiding officer of the parliament of his native Bourgogne, and as a wit praised by Diderot as '*petite tête gaie, ironique et satyrique*', De Brosses had access to many exalted personages of his time; he was presented to Charles Emmanuel III in Turin, to Pope Clement XII in Rome, and to Charles III in Naples. It was no doubt due to the last of these audiences that he was permitted to inspect the excavations.

If ever a writer stood to profit from such an experience, that writer was Charles de Brosses, who was so interested in the ancients that he spent years trying to reconstruct the lost portions of Sallust's *Roman History*, enterprising enough to have just risked his life exploring Mount Vesuvius (although he was so small of stature as to be almost physically handicapped), sufficiently well connected to be given a private tour by the Marchese Marcello Venuti, the King's own antiquary, and so fascinated by Italy that he learned the Neapolitan dialect—which he despised otherwise—merely in order to do full justice to the operas performed at the San Carlo: enough of a scholar to contribute to the *Encyclopédie* and at the same time enough of a man of action to brave the *mofeta*, the acrid, noxious fumes entrapped by the eruption of A.D. 79 which could still do permanent damage to an unwary visitor's lungs. Yet as one compares the account of his ascent of Vesuvius with that of the descent into Herculaneum, one can hardly believe that they were written by the same man and within a few days of one another. The *Excursion au Vésuve* and the *Mémoire sur le Vésuve* addressed to Buffon are spirited little essays by a born *causeur*, full of wit, grace, and lively imagery, in which the periodic emission of lava is likened to milk rising in a pot and boiling over onto the stove, and Monte Somma, to the Roman Coliseum with its partially collapsed shell; when the author, exhausted and satisfied that he has seen all there is to see, finally takes leave of the mountain, he does so 'with the solemn promise never to return for a second visit'.[3] By contrast, the *Mémoire sur la ville souterraine d'Herculée* and that on the Herculanean antiquities are listless descriptions of the amphitheatre and of some works of art, such as the painting of Chiron and Achilles, which were to be commented upon by every later tourist. They quite lack the personal touch which makes the other letters so interesting; indeed, these pages conjure up the Chaplinesque vision of a little man named Charles who was so unceremoniously hustled through the dank corridors that he could do little more than lament that 'they did not let me see everything', 'the people who show these treasures are sullen and terribly jealous', and 'I wish I had had the time' to copy this or that inscription.[4] A pity, because De Brosses was not only a fine writer but a prophet who foretold, by an extraordinary feat of the imagination and at a time when the work had barely begun, a possibility which it took two centuries to implement. 'No doubt many other things of great interest will be discovered in the future,' he wrote from Rome on November 28, 1739, 'especially if the work is managed better than it has been in the past. If everything that has been brought to light were to be nicely arranged, we would surely have the most unusual collection of antiquities that could possibly be assembled.'

If Herculaneum had made its French debut in a minor key, it made a grand entrance into English literature. On the evening of June 14, 1740, Horace Walpole sat down in a Neapolitan inn to tell Richard West, who had stayed behind in England, about his visit to the site:

'. . . You remember in Titus' time there were several cities destroyed by an eruption of Vesuvius, attended with an earthquake. Well, this was one of them, not very considerable, and then called Herculaneum. Above it has since been built Portici, about three miles from Naples, where the king has a villa. This under-ground city is perhaps one of the noblest curiosities that has ever been discovered. It was found out by chance, about a year and a half ago. They began digging, they found statues; they dug further, they found more. Since that they have made a very considerable progress, and find continually. You may walk the compass of a mile; but by the misfortune of the modern town being overhead [the town, actually, was not Portici but Resina], they are obliged to proceed with great caution, lest they destroy both one and t'other. By this occasion the path is very narrow, just wide enough and high enough for one man to walk upright. They have hollowed, as they found it easiest to work, and have carried their streets not exactly where were the ancient ones, but sometimes before houses, sometimes through them. You would imagine that all the fabrics were crushed together; on the contrary, except some columns, they have found all the edifices standing upright in their proper situation. There is one inside of a temple quite perfect, with the middle arch, two columns, and two pilasters. It is built of brick plastered over, and painted with architecture: almost all the insides of houses are in the same manner; and, what is very particular, the general ground of all the painting is red [although the description is of Herculaneum, the colour has since become famous as 'Pompeiian red']. Besides this temple, they make out very plainly an amphitheatre: the stairs, of white marble, and the seats are very perfect; the inside was painted in the same colour with the private houses, and great part cased with white marble. They have found among other things some fine statues, some human bones, some rice, medals, and a few paintings extremely fine. These latter are preferred to all the ancient paintings that have ever been discovered. We have not seen them yet, as they are kept in the King's apartment, whither all these curiosities are transplanted; and 'tis difficult to see them— but we shall. I forgot to tell you, that in several places the beams of the houses remain, but burnt to charcoal; so little damaged that they retain visibly the grain of the wood, but upon touching crumble to ashes . . .

There might certainly be collected great light from this reservoir of antiquities, if a man of learning had the inspection of it; if he directed the working, and would make a journal of the discoveries. But I believe there is no judicious choice made of directors. There is nothing of the kind known in the world; I mean a Roman city entire of that age, and that has not been corrupted with modern repairs. Besides scrutinizing this very carefully, I should be inclined to search for the remains of the other towns that were partners with this in the general ruin [Did Walpole not know, or did he consider it unnecessary to mention that the largest and by far the most important of these towns was Pompeii?]. 'Tis certainly an advantage to the learned world, that this has been laid up so long. Most of the discoveries in Rome were made in a barbarous age, where they only ransacked the ruins in quest of treasure, and had no regard to the form and being of the building; or to any circumstances that might give light into its use and history. I shall finish this long account with a passage which Gray has observed in Statius, and which directly pictures out this latent city:

Haec ego Chalcidicis ad te, Marcelle, sonabam . . . populusque premi? Adieu! my dear West! and believe me yours ever.'[5]

It is only at the end of this breathless letter that Walpole reverts to the stance which was habitual with him on the Grand Tour: that of the Prime Minister's son whose journey was cushioned with all the comforts of the age and smoothed by introductions to everyone who counted. The world was Walpole's oyster, to be explored at will, and Herculaneum a pearl which he chanced to find in it. At the same time, the distance between the 'I' who inspects what 'they' had dug up, was unsurmountable because the closer examination of this pearl was not a gentleman's but a scholar's task.

The scholar, as it happened, was at the gentleman's side. Thomas Gray had joined Walpole on the tour as his guest, and as Walpole somewhat superciliously informed their mutual friend Ashton, 'his travels [had] really improved him'. Poor Gray, who was totally dependent on Walpole for his support, had no choice but to let himself be 'improved' through visiting the museums and monuments of Florence while his worldly friend acquired a mistress and danced through the carnival parties given by his distant cousin, Horace Mann, the resident English minister . . . However, by the time the two friends reached Herculaneum, Gray's 'vile employment' of cataloguing everything they saw proved to be very useful. His enumeration, also in letter form, of the discoveries which had been made is too detailed to be reproduced here. It shares with Walpole's account an air of astonishment 'that this has been laid up so long', some annoyance that 'the work is unhappily under the direction of Spaniards, people of no taste or erudition, so that the workmen dig, as chance directs them, wherever they find the ground easiest to work',[6] and the quotation from Statius. (Beginning with Montaigne, the antiquities and customs of Italy offered travellers among other things also the opportunity of calling upon their knowledge of the ancient writers, less from vanity than from the desire to close a circle by seeing concretely confirmed what had been mere intimations of antiquity acquired in school. Among the English, especially, this habit of considering the sights of Italy as a tangible Q.E.D. of previously gained erudition had been reinforced by Joseph Addison's *Remarks on the Several Parts of Italy, etc. in the Years 1701–3* and the younger Jonathan Richardson's *Account of the Statues, Bas-Reliefs, Drawings and Pictures in Italy, France etc.* of 1722.)

Herculaneum played almost no further role in the lives and works of these two men who went on to become, respectively, the greatest letter-writer and a minor poet in English literature. Yet while it lasted, their interest in the excavations enhanced the enthusiasm which the newly-founded Society of Dilettanti and other groups and individuals of classicist orientation had already engendered in England. Nor did much time elapse before others added their observations to those of Walpole and Gray. In 1750, Wickes Skurray translated Venuti's description of Herculaneum; in 1756, there appeared English versions of De Brosses' *Lettre sur l'état actuel de la ville souterraine d'Herculée etc.* and of Bellicard's *Observations sur les antiquités d'Herculaneum*, and 1762 saw the publication of the first volume of Stuart and Revett's *Antiquities of Athens Measured and Delineated*, Greece, Palmyra, and Paestum having meanwhile joined Campania as the hunting grounds of amateur archae-ologists. Eleven years before, Lady Featherstonhaugh—fittingly enough, also the first of her sex to have climbed Mont Cenis—had been the first woman to compile a report on Herculaneum; it was later read before the Royal Society (by her brother, in order not to violate the statutes) and incorporated into the *Transactions* of that misogynist assembly.

Walpole himself, of course, soon turned 'Gothic' with a vengeance, in writing *The Castle of Otranto* and in building Strawberry Hill. But it was, in any case, in the arts rather than in literature that the re-discovery of Herculaneum, soon to be overshadowed by that of

Pompeii, first bore fruit. In the second half of the eighteenth century, Pompeiian motifs became as distinct a thread in the fabric of Neoclassicism as *chinoiserie* had been in that of the Rococo. This Pompeiian fashion, perhaps the last really cosmopolitan fashion in the decorative arts, eventually extended from the Syon House in Isleworth to the Czernin Palais in Vienna, and indeed from Catherine's Tsarskoe Selo to Jefferson's Monticello. Many of its exponents had studied in Rome and visited the excavations: Clérisseau, Robert Adam, Chalgrin, Giambattista Piranesi, Ingres, David, Canova. Others, like Wedgwood, Böttger, and Schinkel, had acquired the Pompeiian component of their aesthetic second-hand and therefore imperfectly; Wedgwood's famous 'Etruria', for example, has nothing Etruscan about it and might have been more correctly called 'Pompeiia'. The specifically Pompeiian thread—characterized, within neoclassicism as a whole, by stucco decoration, a predilection for cameos and medallions indebted to Hellenic and Hellenistic motifs, and the use of candelabra—was not complemented by a corresponding thread in the *literary* tapestry of the period because literature had not been among the arts of which such splendid examples had been found in Campania. De Brosses, Walpole, Gray, and such lesser figures as the Comte de Caylus, Quatremère de Quincy, or the travel writers Duclos, Lalande, and Dupaty had merely helped to give a first impulse to this fashion. Much time still had to elapse before Schiller, Madame de Staël, and Leopardi could raise the Pompeiian theme from the descriptive to the creative level and establish it as a viable literary subject in *Pompeji und Herkulanum*, *Corinne*, and *La Ginestra*. Before these works could be written, and for that matter before Keats could create his *Ode on a Grecian Urn* or Shelley *Prometheus Unbound*, a catalyst was needed to activate these varied elements and to combine them into an organic whole. By one of the extraordinary coincidences in which the posthumous history of the two cities is so rich, that catalyst now appeared in the person of a cobbler's son in an obscure Prussian village.

'The only way for us to become great, and if possible inimitable, lies in imitating the Greeks'—with this paradoxical statement in his *Gedanken über die Nachahmung der griechischen Werke in der Malerei und Bildhauerkunst* (*Thoughts on the Imitation of Greek Works, etc.*, 1755), Johann Joachim Winckelmann advocated not the slavish copying of the ancients but a re-creation, with an ethos and in a state of mind comparable to those of Greeks, of the artistic practices of classical antiquity. Modern artists, he believed, and especially those of Germany, can realize their potential only if they let themselves be inspired by the Greeks, who had created, naturally and spontaneously, works characterized by 'Noble Simplicity and Quiet Grandeur'. These traits of '*edle Einfalt und stille Grösse*' are the hallmark of the great works of the fifth and fourth centuries B.C., of the period of Phidias, Polyclitus, and Praxiteles. The examination of the works of these masters produces in the viewer more than a vaguely pleasing 'impression': it affects him as an educational, indeed as a moral force in cleansing him of imperfections of the spirit and the impurities of ephemeral fashion. In the young, in particular, it encourages a lifelong receptivity to what is genuine and great. Classical art raises the beholder to an altogether higher sphere, and Winckelmann's reaction to the 'Apollo Belvedere'— 'I forget all else over the sight of this miraculous work of art and assume a more exalted position myself in order to be worthy of this sight'—has since been echoed by many others who similarly felt the obligation placed upon them by Perfection Beheld; thus Rilke has the poem *Archäischer Torso Apollos* end in the reflection 'You must change your life' . . . '*Du musst dein Leben ändern*'.

This didactic function of great art presupposes the existence of a rather precise scale of aesthetic valuation. Clearly, one cannot formulate and hand down to posterity an ideal of beauty without first enumerating and interpreting its components: simplicity and grandeur, a harmony based on the avoidance of extremes, and whatever else they may be; for according to Winckelmann, 'It is not enough to say that something is beautiful. One should also know to what extent and for what reason it is so.' He accordingly proceeded to define the Greek ideal of beauty in a number of works ranging from the *Beschreibung des Torso im Belvedere zu Rom* (*Description of the Belvedere Torso in Rome*) in which praise of the work as a whole is heightened by his evocation of such of Hercules' deeds as occurred to him on beholding the statue, to the several sections of *Geschichte der Kunst des Altertums* (*History of Ancient*

Art, 1764), in which an account of the ethnic, climatic, and social factors connected with the unfolding of Greek art leads up to the central fourth chapter with its masterful analysis of the rise and fall of Greek classicism, of its separate styles, and of its mechanical and technical aspects in regard to workmanship and materials. Roman art, on the other hand, and to a large extent also the later art of Italy and France, are second-rate, derivative at best but more often than not actually detrimental to the striving for perfection. Raphael, to be sure, was a creator of classical works and as such worthy of being placed by the side of the ancients; but Michelangelo is already disharmonious, full of unresolved tensions and leaning toward extreme solutions, and Bernini altogether a 'corruptor of art'. Neither the Roman Baroque nor the Parisian Rococo lie on the road to a classically oriented art; they represent not detours but dead ends. This road does however lead through the remains of ancient Rome, and through Paestum, Pompeii, and Herculaneum, where so many examples of the best Greek works are to be found.

These and others of Winckelmann's views, revolutionary at the time but long since accepted (despite their derivation from an overly narrow view of classical Greece) among the canons of traditionalist European aesthetics, would not have prevailed so quickly and so completely if they had not been backed by the whole force of his extraordinary personality. Born in the Prussian village of Stendal in 1717, he had managed to acquire a classical education in the face of almost unsurmountable odds. After hard years as a tutor and teacher, he had reached, at thirty-one, the position of vice-principal of a country school. There must have been those who thought that Wincklemann, who had set out in life without the slightest claim to rank or wealth, had done very well; with luck, he might end his days as director of a large institution, perhaps even a *Gymnasium,* in one of the bigger Prussian or Saxon cities. Indeed, it would have been a respectable career for a man who in his youth had been so poor that he once walked to Hamburg in order to buy, and carry home on his back, a cheap set of the classics, and so ambitious that after a day in the classroom, he was wont to read until midnight, sleep a few hours at his desk, and wake up again at four in order to return to his studies of Greek and Latin before meeting his first class of the morning,

Winckelmann, however, marched to a drum of his own, and there is nothing to indicate that he was ever content to be a school teacher. He seems to have detested the work at the time, and later looked back with hatred on the 'years of servitude' spent in explaining the ABC to the scabby children—*grindige Kinder*—of Prussian peasants. His chance came in 1748, when he procured a librarian's job with a former diplomat who had retired to his estates and busied himself with the compilation of a History of the German Empire. For six years, Winckelmann made excerpts from legal chronicles for this work and catalogued the library of his employer, Count Heinrich von Bünau. What free time he had was spent on visits to Dresden, residence of the Kings of Poland and Electors of Saxony, and a major art center. Augustus III had just purchased Raphael's 'Sistine Madonna' (and when it arrived, supposedly pushed back his throne with the words 'Make way for the great Raphael'); the *Antikensaal* also contained the misnamed 'Vestal Virgins' which D'Elboeuf had dug up in Herculaneum. Under the influence of this experience, Wickelmann's search for encyclopedic knowledge, so typical of his century, gradually came to focus on artistic and aesthetic problems.

Among the group of local art lovers, he gained the friendship of C.L. von Hagedorn, the poet's brother and director of the Saxon Art Academies, and of the engraver A.F. Oeser, who eventually moved to Leipzig and became young Goethe's teacher. Also, Count Bünau's hospitality and the reputation of his library attracted a good many visitors, among them the Papal Nuncio to the Court of Saxony and Poland, Alberigo Conte d'Archinto, who was fond of conversing with his host's learned secretary. Although Winckelmann had been brought up a Lutheran, he had been so negligent in his religious observances that he had had to be reprimanded, in his schoolmaster days, for hiding in his prayerbook a copy of Homer which he surreptitiously read during Sunday services. He now began to feel that his faith, far from giving him strength and solace, actually held him back. He had no connections, and the librarian's career offered even less chance of advancement than had that of a teacher. There seemed little prospect

A fresco found at Herculaneum showing Hercules finding is son, Telephos, who is being suckled by a deer. Museo Nazionale, Naples.

6a *Above* Alphonse de Lamartine from a lithograph by Delpech.

6b *Below* Edward Bulwer-Lytton, 1st Baron Lytton, painted by P. F. Poole. National Portrait Gallery, London.

of fulfilling his desire to go to Italy in order to experience at first hand that classical art and civilization of which the sculptures in the *Antikensaal* had given him a tantalizing first glimpse. He was a sound scholar, and had read the *Iliad* and *Odyssey* three times in 1753-4 alone, 'with all the application which such divine works demand'; he was at home in art history, and had recently had the opportunity to acquire some social polish as well and to add Italian, French, and English to his languages. Even while his health was beginning to fail from too much studying, he was hard at work on his first major publication, *Thoughts on the Imitation of the Greek Works*, which contained an enthusiastic description of the 'Vestal Virgins'. In short, Winckelmann had done all that could possibly be expected by way of preparing himself for what he felt to be his mission in life: proclaiming the exemplariness of classical Greek art to a world awed by the Baroque and enchanted by the Rococo. This mission, however, could only be carried out on classical soil, preferably in Rome which possessed so many art treasures and represented a basis from which the style-setting influence of Paris could be effectively countered. In order to be able to study in Rome it was necessary, and almost essential for one who had no name or means, to be a Roman Catholic. Not only did the Church then directly administer, in the Vatican and elsewhere, most of the great collections; through its dignitaries abroad, it was also able to further many a scholarly or artistic career and to dispense stipends, publishing privileges, letters of introduction, and other bounties of the sort. After several years of hesitation, Wincklemann took the step which was to open this world to him; with Archinto's blessing and in a ceremony presided over by the king's own confessor, he converted to the Roman faith in 1754. This '*changement*', as he called it, was much commented upon at the time and made him many enemies; yet it does not seem to have greatly affected the habits acquired in earlier years. A friend who visited him in Rome reported that the convert himself had told him '*que tout bon fils de l'Eglise Romaine qu'il étoit, il avoit contracté l'habitude de chanter le matin en préparant son déjeuné (veuillent les Saints du Paradis le lui pardonner!) quelques uns de nos bons Cantiques Luthériens.*'[7] The notion of Winckelmann brewing himself a cup of chocolate and manfully intoning his favourite '*Warum soll' ich mich denn grämen*' in the attic of the Villa Albani, while his patron the cardinal was engaged in his own morning devotions downstairs, goes far toward reconciling one to this particular and presumably inevitable conversion.

Although he published it anonymously, Winckelmann had been far-sighted enough to dedicate his *Thoughts on the Imitation of the Greek Works* to Augustus III. When the latter saw the book, he is said to have promised to see to it that 'this fish shall be put in the water that is right for him'. The right habitat in this case, of course, was Italy, and Winckelmann accordingly set out for Rome in September 1755, with a modest grant in return for which he was to keep the court in Dresden informed about the excavations which Augustus' son-in-law, the King of the Two Sicilies, had been carrying out in such secrecy at Herculaneum. It was an undertaking which he faithfully executed in his letters to Lodovico Bianconi, the royal physician who had done much to smoothe his path.

At the age of thirty-eight Winckelmann was thus able, at long last, to bring to bear on his surroundings the wisdom and skills gathered in the hard years of preparation. He lost no time in establishing himself in Rome, in part with the help of a fellow convert and protégé of the Saxon court, the painter Anton Raphael Mengs who enjoyed a considerable reputation in his time as '*Premier Peintre du Roi de Pologne*'. Their friendship lasted a decade, until Winckelmann, whose aesthetic ideal of the hermaphrodite was enhanced by some homoerotic tendencies in his own make-up, became infatuated with Mengs' wife and took it into his head to announce, with understandable pride, that he had 'finally' managed to fall in love with a woman . . . By then, he had outgrown his need for advice in coping with the artistic and social topography of the Eternal City. He was in fact well on the way toward becoming an institution himself, a spiritual landmark of eighteenth-century Rome, and it is well that we should look on him for a moment in this capacity before accompanying him to Portici, Pompeii, and Herculaneum. It was in Rome and in the years 1755–68 that he wrote the works in which he refined and applied the tenets first set forth in *Thoughts on the Imitation of the Greek Works*: the *History of Ancient Art*, the unfinished *Monumenti antichi inediti* with (partly counterfeit) plates by Giovanni Battista Casanova, the redoubtable Giacomo's younger brother, and a number of smaller publications in the manner of the *Description of the Belvedere Torso in Rome*. At the same time he acted as secretary and companion to Alessandro Cardinal Albani, into whose palatial villa on the Quirinal he had moved in April 1759, and filled some scholarly and honorary positions as a member of the British Society of Antiquaries and of the Accademia di Cortona (along with what came to be the Pompeiian fashion, that of *etruscheria* also flourished in those days) and other Italian academies, as Superintendent of Antiquaries in Rome—it was to this distinction that he owed his title of 'President'—and as *Scriptor Linguae Teutonicae* in the Vatican Library.

A man of such knowledge and standing was inevitably sought after as a guide. Winckelmann did the honours of the city to many of his friends, some of whom later gained a modest reputation of their own like K. and J.H. Fuessli, J.H. von Riedesel, and the Usteri brothers of Zurich, and to some important personages as well. He showed the sights of Rome to one of the Ducs de LaRochefoucauld, to Lord Baltimore, and to the Duke of York (brother of George III, and in Winckelmann's opinion 'the greatest princely ass I know, no credit to his rank or country'). It was inevitable also that other sovereigns should vie with the Princes of the Church in bidding for the services of this savant whom Diderot could compare, in the *Salon de 1765*, with the great Jean-Jacques himself. Joseph II of Austria received him in Vienna in 1768 and bestowed on him so many honours that he unwittingly helped bring about his death; years before, Frederick the Great had tried to lure his erstwhile subject back to Prussia, and the negotiations were well advanced when the Francophile King, incensed at Winckelmann's demand of a salary of 2,000 Taler, terminated them with the remark that 'one thousand Taler are quite sufficient for a German'. By then, Winckelmann himself had reconsidered: 'I shudder from head to foot,' he wrote to L. Usteri, 'to think of Prussian despotism and of the royal slave driver, who will yet make that land cursed by Nature and covered with Lybian sands, into an object of universal destestation . . . *meglio farsi Turco circonciso che Prussiano.*'

Scholarship has always been a commodity of which the supply tends to exceed the demand, and Winckelmann, too, was courted not only as a classicist and archaeologist but because he possessed, along with his splendid erudition, a variety of lighter skills and interests. Gibbon does not seem to have encountered him, but Boswell praised his 'fine and classical taste', and another English visitor added a characteristic touch in remarking that 'Abbé Winckelmann had not the gaiety or gallantry of a lively French Abbé, but he had ease and good breeding with a sufficient knowledge of the world'.[8] This estimate of Winckelmann's personality is particularly striking if we remember its source: the author and agitator John Wilkes, Member of Parliament and Alderman of the City of London, and coiner of some of the most devastating *bons mots* of that malicious century (it was he who on being warned by the Earl of Sandwich that he would die on the gallows or of disease, replied: 'That depends, my lord, on whether I embrace your principles or your mistress')—in short, a man not easily impressed by anyone. Wilkes' point of reference is well chosen because the combination of scholarly and social competence is indeed more common in France than elsewhere. It was, at any rate, almost unknown in eighteenth-century Germany, and the step which Winckelmann so nimbly took from the study into the salon is one which other and greater Germans—Lessing, Herder, Schiller, Beethoven—took either not at all or with dubious grace. Winckelmann's exposure to the mundane life of Rococo Rome, however, laid bare in him not only a worldly but a decidedly rakish streak. One is startled to find that he stood in envious awe of such unreconstructed profligates as Edward Wortley-Montagu and Wilkes himself, and that this learned Abbé who went about in priestly garb discoursing so knowledgeably on classical art, was also one of the first admirers of . . . Fanny Hill. He had read *Memoirs of a Woman of Pleasure* on the occasion of a visit to Horace Mann in 1758, and pronounced it 'the most wanton book the world has ever seen [but written] by a master in the art'. If he lacked the gaiety and gallantry of an *ancien-régime* French Abbé, he was by no means a scholarly recluse.

It is interesting that Wilkes should have commented on his friend's 'breeding'. Winckelmann, of course, had no breeding in that meaning of the word. He was, so to speak, self-bred, and in looking back on his early years must often have felt a schizophrenic sense of unreality; it had its origin in what Goethe was to call his 'unrelenting drive to be esteemed and highly thought of', and no doubt represents a form of arrogance. This is an unpleasant trait, but perhaps a pardonable one in this man who had raised himself, by his own efforts entirely and in an unegalitarian age, to such heights that one of his first biographers, a teacher by the name of J.G. Paalzow who had published a *Character und kurzgefasste Lebensgeschichte des Herrn Präsidenten und Abt W. in Rom (Brief History and Account of the President and Abbé Winckelmann in Rome)* as early as 1764, thought it advisable to preface the work by adducing evidence that its subject was indeed identical with that J.J. Winckelmann who had been, only a few years before, a colleague of his in a Prussian village school. If this famous man now boasted of his fame, especially to those whom he had left behind in anonymity, he also possessed the courage of his convictions. 'The king does not seem to realize,' he commented on Frederick's reluctance to grant him a substantial salary, 'that he would have to pay at least as much to a man who is to exchange Rome for Berlin, and has no need to offer his services to anyone, as to someone who is being called in from St Petersburg and the Arctic Sea [the mathematician Leonhard Euler had just come to Berlin from Russia, to which he eventually returned]. Yet he ought to know that I can be of more use than a mathematician, and that the experience of ten Roman years far outweighs a decade spent in the calculation of parabolic lines, which can be carried on in Tobolsk as well as in Smyrna.'[9] Brave words, not confided to a diary but addressed to a courtier, who for all that the writer knew might well repeat them to the king. Along with the many attributes which he shared with such worldly Abbés as Fénelon and Galiani, Winckelmann evidently had enough steel in him to stand up to the King of Prussia, or for that matter the formidable Lessing who criticized, in his *Laokoon*, Winckelmann's view of Greek art, and of the Laocoön group itself, as imaginative rather than factually sound. One can sympathize with the poet C.F. Weisse's comment on hearing of Winckelmann's death: 'Lessing is the only one who can replace him!'

We have seen that on becoming King of Spain in 1759, Charles III had left the Kingdom of the Two Sicilies to his son Ferdinand, for whom Tanucci acted as regent until he came of age. This did not affect the reluctance of the Neapolitan court to let anyone, least of all a foreigner, examine the objects which were being unearthed. So stringent, in fact, were the royal prohibitions that Giuseppe Canart, who had reconstructed, from the remains of a quadriga, the famous bronze horse of Herculaneum, once led Winckelmann to a closet in his bedroom and explained that not even his wife was allowed to lay eyes on the statue of the god Serapis which was kept there under lock and key. If the court thus resembled the proverbial Immovable Mass, the archaeologist can be likened to the Irresistible Force loosened upon it. Not that he charged blindly; he was, by now, too experienced to believe that the direct way is necessarily the shortest. His first excursion to Portici and Herculaneum, undertaken in 1758, accordingly represented a mere reconnaissance in which he probed the enemy's defences and laid his plans for the attack he was to launch later. Arriving with letters of introduction from Bianconi and Mengs, he proved to be too well-connected a visitor to be turned away at the gate. But he was, at the same time, too prestigious a scholar to be admitted to the premises: his fame as an archaeologist and art historian had preceded him, and the incompetent courtiers in charge of the excavations were intent on keeping him at arm's length in order to protect their sinecures. To be sure, he quickly breached the first line of defence; when the museum staff refused him admittance, he went directly to Tanucci and obtained at least a temporary permit to look around. However, he was not allowed to take notes or visit the site of the excavations, and the celebrated Satyr was not in the museum at all but had been 'borrowed' by Canart. Thus Winckelmann found himself in effect side-tracked to the study of a particular aspect of the excavations: to the deciphering of the papyri which Camillo Paderni, the museum's director, had found in Herculaneum on October 19, 1752. These were badly charred papyrus rolls which disintegrated into dust at the slightest touch. It was quickly established that they were written in Greek, but only one roll, somewhat less carbonized than its fellows, could be partially deciphered; it turned out to be a copy of an already known treatise on music, by the Epicurean philosopher Philodemus, a very minor figure who had lived in Rome in Caesar's time. Scholars all over Europe had meanwhile begun to wonder what the other manuscripts might contain:

Sophocles' lost dramas, perhaps, or works by an author whose very name had been erased by the passing of time? It was therefore imperative that a means of unrolling the papyri be devised quickly. Since the problem transcended Paderni's capacities, the King called in Antonio Piaggio, a Piarist Father and former custodian in the Vatican library who had constructed a complicated machine, a veritable nightmare of pigs' bladders (to provide artificial backing on which the wafer-thin material could be unfolded and glued), winches, and silk thread, by means of which he intended to unroll at a snail's pace the 1,800-odd scraps of manuscript which had meanwhile accumulated in the museum's vault. All suggestions as to speeding up the process, including one involving the use of chemicals in order to achieve an etched reproduction of the text, fell on the deaf ears of Alexius Mazzocchi, an elderly cleric who had been one of the founding members of the Academy of Herculaneum. He had procured for himself the privilege of making a translation of whatever works might eventually be brought to light, and had no intention of letting younger and abler men undercut this monopoly by presenting them with copper plates, which once reproduced could of course be read by anyone with a knowledge of Greek. He had no way of knowing that his worries were groundless; other and better minds, including that of Sir Humphry Davy who spent some frustrating months in the museum in 1819, have since struggled with the papyri, only to find that it was not worth the bother (while Baudelaire, on the other hand, was to base his story *Le jeune enchanteur* precisely on the fictitious deciphering of one of these documents). It was only very recently that Anton Fackelmann of Vienna has discovered, in the regeneration of the sheets through the sap of the papyrus plant, a method which bids fair to solve the problem.

Rebuffed on all sides, Winckelmann made friends with Piaggio and watched him at work. He had meanwhile surreptitiously examined a sufficient number of exhibits—the painting of Chiron and Achilles, the statutes of the Balbi family, some mosaics, vases, and candelabra—to clarify to his satisfaction several questions relating to the sequence of various phases of Greek and Hellenistic art. Through his association with Piaggio he now became an expert in the technical aspects of ancient writing, and in a brilliant feat of creative scholarship reconstructed in his mind the function and development of the *stylus:* the materials of which it was made, the possible shapes it could take, and the precise manner in which it was used for writing and erasing.

His second visit, in early 1762, confirmed him in the suspicion he had harboured even before the exploratory trip of 1758—that the entire project of excavating the buried cities and of preserving and cataloguing their contents was being grossly mismanaged. A total of fifty men had been assigned to the actual digging, but only eight to the most promising site, that of Pompeii, which was to be identified as such on August 20, 1763, through an inscription referring to the *res publica Pompeiianorum;* until then, it had been mistaken for Stabiae. The work gangs were made up of Barbary Pirates captured in the innumerable skirmishes between the Neapolitan and Turkish fleets, and of convicts so tightly chained together that they could barely move, let alone wield a spade with the requisite care and agility. The scene of the excavations shifted back and forth between Herculaneum, Pompeii, and Stabiae (near the modern Castellammare di Stabia), as chance or the court's cupidity dictated; for only one man, Alcubierre's assistant Karl Weber, was motivated by something resembling scientific curiosity. Thus the Villa of Julia Felix, first discovered in 1755, had been left half-unearthed while the diggers hurried on elsewhere; on February 8, 1764 and in Winckelmann's presence, some mosaics by Dioscorides of Samos were found in the deserted edifice, which was then covered up again, as holding no further promise of treasure, and not completely cleared until 1953. The results were predictably uneven. Some splendid works of art were discovered, but much time was also wasted on trivia: a sun dial, examined by Winckelmann but lost since; a small table at which he drank his Lacrima Cristi one evening, in the company of the despised Paderni; some Priapi which the ribald archaeologist described in detail to Bianconi, in a letter of which the first, rather outspokenly anatomical paragraphs are usually suppressed. Taken as a whole, however, the finds stood in no relation to the effort that had been expended, or for that matter, to the anticipation of great discoveries which the Neapolitan court had done nothing to discourage. Winckelmann now decided to take matters into his own hands and to launch a frontal attack by publishing his *Sendschreiben von den Herculanischen Entdek-*

kungen (*Open Letter on the Discoveries made at Herculaneum*, 1762). It was ostensibly addressed to Count Brühl, his companion on this trip, but in reality represented a carefully planned and planted exposé which had been forwarded to the publisher with precise instructions about the copies which were to be sent, with the author's compliments, to art patrons and fellow-scholars in Paris, Vienna, Warsaw, and elsewhere. Naples did not figure on this list of addresses, and for good reason: the author had been warned that the pamphlet would make it almost impossible for him ever to set foot again in the Kingdom of the Two Sicilies.

In this open Letter and the supplementary *Nachrichten von den neuesten Herculanischen Entdeckungen* (*Report on the most recent Excavations at Herculaneum*) addressed to H. Füssli and published in 1764, Winckelmann gave vent to his accumulated ire. He spared no one—neither Paderni nor Alcubierre, the Spanish engineering officer about whom Thomas Gray had complained earlier and whose sins of commission and omission (such as removing, and proudly presenting to the king in a basket, some bronze letters found on a wall in Herculaneum, while neglecting to read and record the inscription in which they had been arranged) now became public knowledge, nor yet Baiardi, that scholarly mountain which had laboured so mightily and given birth to a mouse: not the catalogue expected of him, but the *prodromi* containing his labyrinthine account of the adventures of Hercules. At the same time, Winckelmann gave his readers an idea of the pall of mistrust and suspicion which hung heavily over the scene; in fact, the engraving of Demosthenes' bust which was reproduced at the end of the Open Letter had had to be stealthily sketched by Mengs, in the manner of a detective shadowing a criminal, 'when he found an opportunity to do so' in Portici.

What made the pamphlets so convincing was the fact that they contained, along with the vituperative passages, others in which Winckelmann implicitly demonstrated the loss which accrued to the world of scholarship through the obscurantism of the bureaucrats in Portici and Naples. From what little he had been able to observe, he was able to determine that many of the inhabitants of Pompeii and Herculaneum had left their homes after the earthquake of A.D. 63, and

that the remaining Pompeiians had returned in considerable numbers
after the eruption of A.D. 79 in order to salvage what they could of their
possessions. Many key passages in Vitruvius Pollio and other architectural writers of antiquity, he found, could be fully understood only
now that one was—or ought to be—able to compare, for example, the
large orchestra of the Greek with the smaller one of the Roman theatre
and to reconstruct mentally, *in situ*, the machines used for changing the
scenery within a play. These and similar observations were couched in
Winckelmann's particular blend of scholarly conciseness and sensual
imagery, as in the following passage which was inspired by nothing
more poetic than some pitchers and vases from Herculaneum and yet
illustrates his gift of proceeding deductively from the close examination
of details to the formulation of widely applicable statements on
aesthetics:

'These vessels owe their beauty to their gently curving lines, which
as in beautiful young bodies are not fully grown but still maturing,
so that the eye neither exhausts itself in beholding perfectly shaped
semispherical outlines nor comes up against corners or points. The
sweet sensation conveyed by such lines can be likened to [the touch
of] a soft, tender hand. In the presence of such harmony, our very
thoughts become light and palpable.'

If one visitor, constantly hemmed in by red tape, could so illuminate
the characteristics of ancient pottery and the nature of beauty itself,
what heights might scholarship not attain if the excavations were
opened to scholars from all lands, to measure and copy and meditate
as they pleased? Had not Horace Walpole already observed that 'there
might certainly be collected great light from this reservoir of antiquities,
if a man of learning had the inspection of it; if he directed the working,
and would make a journal of the discoveries?'

Such, no doubt, were the reflections of many who read Winckelmann's reports from Herculaneum. Among these contemporary readers
was the French archaeologist and art collector Anne-Claude-Philippe
de Caylus, who promptly had the *Report on the most recent Excavations*
translated into French in order to give it wider publicity. Like its
predecessor, the Open Letter of 1762, it had attracted little attention at
first because it was written in German, a language which was only just

beginning to be valued as a vehicle for learned communication. But when the Abbé Galiani, secretary to His Sicilian Majesty's ambassador in Paris, gave Sir William Hamilton a copy of the French text to take along to Naples, that Majesty and all his ministers were incensed at what they considered a grave indiscretion on the part of Winckelmann; the latter, in turn, became so apprehensive that he confessed to a friend his fear that 'a beating, if not something worse' would surely await him on his next trip south. Two Neapolitan scholars, stung into making a reply to the accusation of incompetence which had been levelled against them, hastily got out an anonymously published *Giudizio dell'opera dell'Abbate W. intorno alle scoverte di Ercolano* (*Evaluation of the Abbé W.'s Work on the Herculanean Discoveries*, 1765) in which they made fun of him for believing and passing on as gospel 'every scrap of misinformation whispered in his ear by some prisoner or another on the site'.

It was unfortunate that the storm should have broken just then. A period of particularly intensive digging was about to begin, during which several major buildings were found in Pompeii and much incidental information brought to light which enabled scholars to fill in, as it were, the bare shells of these buildings with suggestions of the life that had once pulsated within their walls. In the Temple of Isis, for example, the remains of the eggs and fish were discovered which the priests had been preparing for their meal when they were struck down, and the position in which their bodies were found demonstrated in dramatic detail the story of their thwarted flight. The discovery of the Great Theatre in 1764 confirmed much of what had previously been surmised about the construction and function of these edifices, while that of the adjacent Gladiators' Barracks (1766) furnished the raw material for some particularly poignant reminders of the cruelty of fate: two skeletons were found with their wrists shackled (the men had evidently been in prison and died a horrible death), and elsewhere in the building, the indiscreet visit—if such it was—of a bejewelled woman, whose body was discovered on these pre-eminently masculine premises, showed that these men were not only the victims but to some extent also the heroes of Roman society. This has since been borne out by the Pompeiian graffiti extolling the athletic and amatory prowess of such stalwarts as Auctus (who vanquished fifty foes), Severus (fifty-six victories in the arena), and Celadus, the *suspirium puellarum* who evidently broke as many hearts as his colleagues had cracked skulls. Temporarily banished from the scene of these finds, Winckelmann had to rely on others to keep him abreast of them. One can imagine with what impatience he listened to the Duc de LaRochefoucauld's description of the wonders of the Temple of Isis, and how proudly he forwarded to the painter Clérisseau a sketch which someone had sent him of the Gladiators' Barracks.

It turned out to be an unnecessarily round-about way of exchanging news. The royal displeasure was of short duration, and on the occasion of Winckelmann's last visit the amenities were observed on all sides. As a token of forgiveness, Tanucci presented him with the fifth volume of the *Antichità d'Ercolano*, and Winckelmann on his part undertook to review the publication, containing magnificent reproductions of 120 bronzes in the Portici Museum, in a spirit which for him was downright mellow. To be sure, he never changed his opinion of King Ferdinand, whom he characterized in December of that year as 'a little beast of sixteen' who had only once set foot in the museum and whose greatest pleasure consisted in watching the vivisection of pregnant deer, or of Paderni, 'that fourth-rate draftsman who had been on the point of starving to death in Rome when he was lucky enough to be commissioned to copy the ancient paintings'; Winckelmann, however, was no longer young, and the man who after his arrival in Rome had exulted '*Superavi Te, fortuna!*', had lately been beset by premonitions of disaster. Yet on the face of it all was well, and Mount Vesuvius even treated the distinguished visitor to a spectacular eruption which he watched in the company of the French adventurer d'Hancarville and of his own favourite, the young baron J.H. von Riedesel. A few months later, he was stabbed to death by a robber to whom he had foolishly shown, in Trieste where he was waiting for a ship to take him back to his beloved Rome, the medals and decorations which Maria Theresa and the Chancellor Kaunitz had given him during his triumphal visit to Vienna earlier in 1768.

More than any other man it was this self-made scholar, the founder of scientific archaeology, who put Pompeii and Herculaneum on the

map of localities in which the unfolding of western civilization may
best be observed. What he wrote on the cities makes up only a fraction
of his total work, but the effect of that work as a whole has been truly
incalculable. In England, Winckelmann's credo helped to replace the
Palladian fashion with a genuine Neoclassicism; enhanced by the
archaeologist's own independence of mind and manner, it helped to
bring about in France that identification of Neoclassicism with
Republicanism which characterized the revolutionary and Napoleonic
period; it inspired Italian poets like Vittorio Alfieri and Vincenzo
Monti with renewed pride in their country's creative past, and encouraged American artists like Hiram Powers and Horatio Greenough
to attempt the transplanting of a classically-oriented aesthetic to
the New World. To mention only two details in which Winckelmann's
influence can be seen to this day: it may be argued that men have never
again claimed, as had been the fashion in his youth, that Roman art is
the equal of that of Greece; also, art historians have never since then
ceased to study the few works to which he assigned a seminal function
in the development of aesthetics, such as the four great statues in
the Vatican Belvedere—Laocoön, Torso, Apollo, and the so-called
'Antinoüs'. Along with a handful of other ancient works, these represent the classical ideal in sculpture. Artists can pay homage to that
ideal by imitating or by purposely rejecting it; but since Winckelmann's
time, they cannot be ignorant of it if they want to be taken at all
seriously.

Although many of his compatriots from Lessing to Spengler have
disagreed with him on this or that aspect of ancient life and art,
Winckelmann yet imparted to the nascent classical phase of German
letters an admiration for Ancient Greece which was to transcend
national and temporal boundaries in the works of Goethe, Schiller,
and Hölderlin. Modified by Nietzsche and brought up-to-date by
Burckhardt and others, this legacy, nourished in no small measure by
what Winckelmann had observed in the Campanian cities, has endured
to our time in the writings of Hofmannsthal, George, and Benn.
Beginning in his own time through his works, his contacts with visitors
to Rome, and his correspondence with such writers as Gellert, Nicolai,
Mendelssohn, and Gottsched, Winckelmann's influence on German

literature has been profound; never again, for example, have Germans seriously entertained the notion, prevalent in his youth, that works of intellectual import had to be written in Latin or French. Within this legacy, finally, the archaeologist's figure itself has fascinated Germans from Herder's *Kritische Wälder* through Goethe's *Winckelmann und sein Jahrhundert* to Hauptmann's *Winckelmann* and Bergengruen's *Die letzte Reise*.

Even if many of them later modified their views, countless Germans since the days of J.J.W. Heinse and K.P. Moritz first saw Italy and Pompeii through Winckelmann's eyes. It is indicative that the greatest of these northern visitors and indeed the greatest of all the writers who were significantly affected by their exposure to Pompeii, Johann Wolfgang Goethe, should not only have studied and commented upon Winckelmann's works but oriented himself by means of guidebooks written by his disciples.[10]

Goethe set down the bulk of his impressions of Pompeii and Herculaneum in his *Italienische Reise* (*Italian Journey*, 1816–17):

'As Tischbein and I drove to Pompeii,' we read under the date of March 11, 1787 in the Auden-Mayer translation, 'we saw on every hand many views which we well knew from drawings, but now they were all fitted together into one splendid landscape. Pompeii surprises everyone by its compactness and smallness of scale. The streets are narrow, though straight and provided with pavements, the houses small and windowless—their only light comes from their entrances and open arcades—and even the public buildings, the bench tomb at the town gate, the temple and a villa nearby look more like architectural models or dolls' houses than real buildings.

Considering the distance between Pompeii and Vesuvius, the volcanic debris which buried the city cannot have been driven here, either by the explosive force of the eruption or by a strong wind: my own conjecture is that the stones and ashes must have remained suspended in the air for some time, like clouds, before they descended upon the unfortunate city. To picture more clearly what must have happened historically one should think of a mountain village buried in snow. The spaces between the buildings, and even the buildings themselves, crushed under the weight of the fallen material, were buried and invisible, with perhaps a wall sticking up here and there; sooner or later, people took this mound over and planted vineyards and gardens on it. The mummified city left us with a curious, rather disagreeable impression, but our spirits began to recover as we sat in the pergola of a modest inn looking out over the sea, and ate a frugal meal. The blue sky and the glittering sun enchanted us, and we left hoping that, on some future day, when this little arbour was covered with vine leaves, we would meet there again and enjoy ourselves.'

In the entry for March 13 is found this supplementary passage:

'On Sunday we went to Pompeii again. There have been many disasters in this world, but few which have given so much delight to posterity, and I have seldom seen anything so interesting. The city gate and the avenue of tombs are unusual. There is one tomb of a priestess, shaped like a semicircular bench and with an inscription carved in large letters on its stone back.[11] As I looked over it, I saw the sun setting into the sea.'

Under the date March 18, finally, we find the following:

'We could not put off any longer going to see Herculaneum and the Portici museum of objects excavated there. It is a thousand pities that the site was not excavated methodically by German miners, instead of being casually ransacked as if by brigands, for many noble works of antiquity must have been thereby lost or ruined. We had good letters of recommendation to the museum and were well received, but we were not allowed to make any drawings. Perhaps this made us pay attention all the more closely to what we saw, so that we were all the more vividly transported into the past, when all these objects were part and parcel of their owners' daily life. They quite changed my picture of Pompeii. In my mind's eye its homes now looked both more cramped and more spacious—more cramped because I now saw them crowded with objects, and more spacious because these objects were not made merely for use but were decorated with such art and grace that they enlarged and refreshed the mind in a way that the physical space of even the largest room cannot do.

There was one beautiful jar, for example, with an exquisitely wrought rim which, on closer inspection, turned out to be two hinged semicircular handles, by which the vessel could be lifted and carried with ease. The lamps are decorated with as many masks and scrolls of foliage as they have wicks, so that each flame illuminates a different work of art. There were high, slender bronze pedestals, evidently intended as lamp stands. The lamps which were suspended from the ceiling were hung with all sorts of cunningly wrought figures which surprise and delight the eye as they swing and dangle. We followed the custodians from room to room, trying to enjoy and learn as much as possible in the little time we had. We hope to come back.'

These observations were later supplemented by passages in the historical sections of the *Farbenlehre* and in *Winckelmann und sein Jahrhundert* and other incidental essays as well as in letters to Boisserée, Iken, Zelter, Knebel, Cotta, and August von Goethe. They may be summarized by saying that Goethe's interest in the excavations found no reflection in any of the major works and may therefore appear somewhat ephemeral. Yet the intriguing sentence 'I have seldom seen anything so interesting', by a writer who in his mature years was not given to exaggeration, makes it worthwhile to enter into the spirit of these comments and to check them against certain traits and idiosyncracies of Goethe's, such as his uncommon, not to say uncanny instinct for all that is important and potentially productive, for 'the shape of things to come'. Furthermore, it was in Goethe's *Italian Journey* that the Pompeiian motif, which we have hitherto encountered chiefly in epistolary and scholarly writing, first gained a place in a major work by a major writer: a place in world literature.

What strikes one first of all is that the comments are framed by a description of the natural setting. The first passage begins with 'many views which we knew well from drawings' and ends with 'the blue sky and the glittering sea'. The salient point is not the weaving of landscape and architecture into an image pleasing to eye (a commonplace discovery of visitors to Italy), but the supremacy of the former over the latter: the preponderance of nature over a classical antiquity which revealed itself to Goethe not as an example of *edle Einfalt und stille*

The Harpist (Madame de Staël) by Elizabeth Vigée-
Lebrun.

8a *Above* Vesuvius erupting on December 22, 1817, seen
from Naples. After a watercolour.

8b *Below* The Temple of Isis, Pompeii, 1788; engraving by
Francesco Piranesi. British Museum, London.

Grösse, but as a depressing conglomeration of half-destroyed dwellings. A few days later, in Paestum, the poet was to react differently; *those* temples did correspond to Winckelmann's definition, and Goethe was as much prepared for them as he had been for the Pompeiian landscape which he already 'knew well from drawings'. Although the interplay of nature and art is rather more impressive at Paestum than in Pompeii, Goethe found the landscape there 'very unpicturesque', while the temples filled him with 'stupefaction'. (His guide in Paestum, of course, was no longer Wilhelm Tischbein, the experienced Cicerone whose enthusiasm for the Naples region surely coloured Goethe's own attitude, but the subaltern C.H. Kniep, whom the poet, gifted as he was in rare measure with the knack of getting the most out of his associates, used as the modern tourist might use a camera: he set him to work sketching the temples.)

Men have sought and found the most diverse experiences in the Mediterranean lands. They have discovered art and music there among a congenial people, regained their health, studied the remnants of past civilizations, fallen in love, or merely escaped from their humdrum daily lives in the North. Goethe did all of this, and something else besides. Few if any visitors have returned from these enchanted regions with such gains in their understanding of the physical universe as came to Goethe in Italy. In a lesser man, this might seem a woefully unartistic, one is inclined to say 'unromantic' result of such a voyage. Yet Goethe, who in Venice had paid less attention to St Mark's than to the bone structure of a sheep's skull which he chanced to find on the Lido, would not have been true to himself if he had not buttressed his aesthetic speculations with a scientific one. How sound the latter is in regard to the Great Eruption, i.e., how valid the hypothesis that the lapilli and ashes which fell on Pompeii were not carried there by the wind or the centrifugal force of the eruption but hovered in the atmosphere before precipitating, did not become fully evident until March 18, 1944. On that date, Mount Vesuvius re-enacted on a small scale its performance of August 24, 79 by sending aloft, on a calm day, ashes which hovered in the air for hours before descending on Pompeii but not on Herculaneum (which, it will be remembered, had been enveloped not by fiery ashes but by a mud avalanche).

6

If Goethe knew Pliny's letters to Tacitus, he does not refer to them here, on the scene of the disaster; the Pliny mentioned elsewhere in the *Italian Journey* is the Elder. In any event, Goethe and De Brosses stand apart from the other early visitors to the excavations as the only ones who mentally reconstructed the course of the catastrophe in a manner consonant both with Pliny's eyewitness account and with the meteorological conditions which must have prevailed at the time. It is odd that it should have been Goethe, a poet and primarily a lyric poet, who undertook this reconstruction which one would rather have expected of a 'man of action'. Such a man did, in fact, visit Pompeii not long after him. But Horatio Lord Nelson, on whose meteorological acumen the fate of Europe depended more than once, had eyes only for his companion, the bewitching Emma—the same Lady Hamilton whom Goethe also met and admired, without letting himself be distracted for a moment from his interest in the people, the art, and the climate of the region.

This reconstruction is the more remarkable if one considers another aspect of Goethe's reaction to Pompeii. Given his 'Neptunic' rather than 'Volcanic' concept of the forces of Nature, one is impressed by how strongly he inclined toward the former principle on his visit to this, the most volcanic region he ever set foot in. He did climb Vesuvius three times, in a state of mind balanced between athletic bravado and scientific curiosity; but he always, so to speak, inwardly rejected the mountain, and believed that he was imposing on Tischbein when the latter accompanied him to the top, 'reluctantly' as the poet observed, 'but out of loyal fellowship'. The eeriness of the phenomenon and its existential terror hardly touched him and did not call forth from his imagination the nightmarish visions it evoked from others.

'It was a rough, narrow trail,' wrote Mark Twain, 'and led over an old lava-flow—a black ocean which was tumbled into a thousand fantastic shapes—a wild chaos of ruin, desolation and barrenness—a wilderness of billowy upheavals, of furious whirlpools, of miniature mountains rent asunder—of gnarled and knotted, wrinkled and twisted masses of blackness that mimicked branching roots, great vines, trunks of trees, all interlaced and mingled together; and all these weird shapes, all this turbulent panorama, all this stormy, far-reaching waste of blackness, with its thrilling suggestiveness of life, of action, of boiling, surging, furious motion, was petrified!'[12]

In Goethe's description one searches in vain for the Greek term *chaos*, which lives on in the Western languages and instinctively occurred in this locality to Chateaubriand and Shelley and Hebbel and Mark Twain and Juan Valera; there is no hint, in Goethe's lines, of the 'horror and oppression which gripped Dickens, or the reminiscences of Dante's *Inferno* which Vesuvius triggered in Madame de Staël, in Carl Gustav Carus, and in Blasco-Ibáñez. Goethe, more of a scientist than any of these, took this evidence of the destructive forces of nature very much in his stride and did not bother to describe in any detail the power which had obliterated the cities. With the deletion of only a few words in his account, one might think that they had fallen victim to a landslide or a flood.

Linked to the volcanic is another principle, the ramifications of which Goethe endeavoured to mitigate wherever possible in life and art: the tragic. It would be an exaggeration to state that the fate of Pompeii and Herculaneum had not touched him at all; but it is strange, and yet consistent with his personality, that he should barely mention this aspect and even manage to extract from it some good. In a letter to K.B. Cotta we read:

'The eager connoisseur who examines with delight the excavations at Pompeii and Herculaneum is . . . struck by the painful thought that so much happiness had to be erased by a single upheaval of nature in order to deposit and preserve for him such treasures.'

This teleological view is very much the poet's own. One would be hard put to find a more restrained way of paraphrasing the annihilation of two flourishing cities and the painful death of so many men, women and children whose earthly pilgrimage, one would like to believe, must have served some purpose in the divine scheme of things beyond that of adding to our knowledge and appreciation of classical antiquity. For Goethe, however, the death of Pompeii epitomized not the transitoriness of life but the immortality of art. His comments therefore contain neither an accusation against fate, as does Martial's epigram, nor an attempt to re-live the life of the ancients on an existential rather than antiquarian basis, in the manner of Bulwer-Lytton, Baudelaire, Gautier,

Jensen, and so many others. If this lack of emotional involvement is typically Goethean, another attitude of the poet's is quite atypical: his lament that 'it is a thousand pities that the site was not excavated methodically by German miners'. In the light of the conditions then prevailing on that site, the remark must not be taken as an instance of chauvinism—a sentiment quite foreign to Goethe—but as a thought which had surely occurred to many non-Germans as well.

The eighteenth-century visitor, of course, came away from the cities with an impression very unlike that held by the modern sightseer. Not only were most of the patrician dwellings (the House of the Vettii, House of the Menander, Villa of the Mysteries, etc.) still waiting to be restored to the light of day, so that the telescoped image suggested by such terms as 'smallness . . . narrow . . . dolls' houses . . . mummified . . . curious and rather disagreeable' is reflected also in other descriptions of the time; for example by Goethe's compatriot J.G. Seume who expressed both dimensions of Pompeii in the laconic observation that 'the ancients, after all, did live in a somewhat confined space; nevertheless, the city as a whole must have been magnificent enough'[13]; it must also be remembered that architectural greatness is so subjective a term that Gray could call Versailles 'a lumber of littleness' and Shelley could consider St Peter's in Rome, Christendom's biggest church, as 'petty on a small scale'. No doubt Goethe, as well as Seume, Chateaubriand and others who were troubled by the smallness of Pompiian houses, were taken aback to find that the actual dimensions of these buildings stood in no relation to their own mental image of Roman grandeur. The present practice of leaving frescoes, sculptures, and utensils in place and merely protecting them against the climate could not then be followed because King Ferdinand preferred to inspect his treasures in comfort, in the museums of Portici and Naples. No one had yet thought of replanting the peristyles and gardens with the flowers which had once bloomed there; neither the wine reservoirs of Boscoreale nor the surgical instruments had been discovered, and little was known about the main Pompeiian trades. The aura of paralysis, the impression of a city arrested at the moment of death and preserved like a fly in amber, must have been stronger than it is today. Under these circumstances, Goethe's fascination with the jars and lamps in the museum is truly prophetic because domestic objects of this nature, little regarded when they were first found, mean more to us now than do the sculptures which have been brought to light in Pompeii. Although there are a few fine pieces among them, they cannot equal what has been found elsewhere. Here again, one admires Goethe's intuition of what was to come. He seems to have anticipated the change which the discovery of Pompeii and Herculaneum brought about in our concept of classical antiquity: whereas we once saw the ancients in the harsh glare of the heroic epic they now appear to us, as often as not, in the gentler light of their domestic concerns.

It is likely that Goethe had grasped this instinctively and, spoilt as he was in this respect by his Roman sojourn, now purposely neglected sculpture in favour of painting, an art of which Pompeii and Herculaneum have indeed given us unique examples. (Until the discovery of the Campanian cities, remains of ancient painting had been exceedingly rare, not much more being known than the 'Aldobrandini Marriage' and Fabullus' ornamental *grotteschi* on the Palatine.) The account in the *Italian Journey*, the brief essay *On Arabesques*, the biographical sketch of Philipp Hackert and references in the Didactic as well as Historical Part of the *Farbenlehre* (*Theory of Colours*) all attest to the poet's admiration for the Pompeiian frescoes, among which the 'elegant and extraordinarily delicate' forms of the Centaurs and Bacchantes from the so-called Villa of Cicero called forth his especial praise. How he would have reacted to Pompeiian art in the grand manner such as it was discovered later, to the frescoes in the Villa of the Mysteries or the bust of Lucius Caecilius Jucundus or the 'Battle of Alexander'—which he only knew from a drawing, although his son August had been present at the discovery of the House of the Faun, called 'Casa di Goethe' in his honour—is a matter of conjecture which need not detain us here. Transcending mere wit and elegance, these works attain the level of individualization and might well have prompted Goethe to revise his ideas about Pompeiian art as a whole.

More legitimate, perhaps, is another conjecture. What would have happened if Goethe had visited the cities at that time, but under more favourable circumstances? The modern technique of making casts of the forms of victims, in which the vacuum left by the decayed body is filled with a gypsum-like substance which is then allowed to harden, was not invented until the 1860's; it has since preserved for us some of the most affecting of all records of the catastrophe, such as the writhing form of the dog of Vesonius Primus, petrified in its death agony. But already in Goethe's time some bodies had been recovered, and in a few instances it had been possible to make a cast of their form, like that of the young woman's bosom which plays so suggestive a rôle in Gautier's *'Arria Marcella'*. If Goethe had been shown some of the bodies which had been preserved even then, or permitted to watch the exhumation of a corpse, the metaphysical impact of such an experience may well have counterbalanced the attitude of *ars longa, vita brevis* which characterizes his view of Pompeii. To that end he would have had to travel not incognito but under his own name, so famous in Italy at that period. The authorities may well have laid on for him one of the 'counterfeit digs' which were prepared for Joseph II and Francis I of Austria, Marie Louise, Leopold I of Belgium, Pope Pius IX, the young Queen Victoria, and sundry other crowned or otherwise prominent heads. A freshly discovered edifice which had been thoughtfully filled with coins or statutuary was simply re-buried in order to be discovered once more, with well-rehearsed cries if surprise, in the honoured guest's presence. Joseph II and some others saw through the farce, but preferred to keep their knowledge to themselves for the time being; others took it at face value, like the King of Württemberg in whose presence the House of the Surgeon was re-re-rediscovered, for the third time since its disappearance in 79, on October 31, 1818. One wonders how Goethe would have reacted to this game: whether he would have seen through it, and above all, whether his attendance during the physical act of digging might have added a dynamic dimension to the elegiac mood which customarily overtakes the museum visitor and which the poet himself defined as 'curious and rather disagreeable'.

Another experience which he was not destined to have was a discussion with the director of the excavations. When the young Edward Bulwer, for example, visited Pompeii in 1833, he was loath to accompany his friends on what threatened to turn into yet another bit of obligatory sightseeing. Letting the others go ahead with the guide, he sat down in order to await the time when they could all return to the hotel. The archaeologist Antonio Bonucci noticed the *milord inglese* disconsolately perched on a stone bench, and involved him in a conversation which was to leave its mark on the history of the novel. It is as tempting to picture Goethe in this situation as it is to enlarge on the fact that the other ancient city which lives on in Man's imagination on account of the manner in which it died, namely Troy, owes its immortality not to the archaeologist's spade but to the poet's lyre. It is a temptation which we shall resist in favour of the simple observation that Goethe did *not* make the acquaintance of Francesco La Vega, the able director of the excavations at the time of his visit, and nonetheless observed and divined in Pompeii a number of details which did not reveal themselves fully to others until much later.

For Goethe, Pompeii came to symbolize in the course of time the greatest of his loves: that for classical antiquity, which forms the common denominator of all the protean shapes of his personality. He had been captivated by the town at the age of thirty-eight; forty years later, the visit of a young friend just returned from there drew forth from him the most touching of his many acknowledgements of debt to the ancients. The visitor, the artist Wilhelm Zahn, has left a report of this interlude which deserves to be reproduced, as the best description ever given of Goethe *en famille* and as an example of the spell which Pompeii casts not only over innumerable anonymous travellers, but over some truly extraordinary men.

'I was still an unknown young man when I came through Weimar on the way to Berlin, on September 7, 1827. All my thoughts revolved around Goethe, and I decided to call on the Great Man. However, it was no easy task to get to him; besieged as he was by visitors every day, he kept secluded. The painter and author August Kopisch, discoverer of the Blue Grotto at Capri, told me that he had written the poet a long letter requesting an interview, but received no reply. Another acquaintance, whose name escapes me, had actually made his way up to the house and timidly sneaked into the yard, hoping to find a servant. But all he encountered were two boys, the poet's grandsons, running about wildly and creating an uproar. Suddenly, a window opened, and the object of his desires leaned out. "For the last time will you rascals keep quiet!" he shouted, eyes aflame and in a leonine voice, and slammed the window shut. The boys calmed down, and my friend stole away frightened. Undaunted by these inauspicious episodes, I cheerfully set out on my way, even though I had neither a reputation to recommend me nor the slightest introduction.

In the hall I gave my name to a manservant: "Zahn. Painter and architect." "Painter and architect," the man replied, looking me over dubiously. "Tell His Excellency that I have just returned from Italy." "Returned from Italy," he repeated mechanically, and left. When he came back, he asked me to follow him . . . to a stately drawing-room.

Shortly afterwards, Goethe entered. It has been said a thousand times that his appearance and bearing were Olympian, and truly no one could deny that the man who now stood before me had no equal. Old age merely accentuated the power of his tall, strong, and venerable figure. Two large brown eyes sparkled under the tremendous forehead, and the bronze-hued face bore the stamp of a noble mind. He made me sit down facing him, and asked in his expressive, well-modulated voice which now and then betrayed traces of Frankfurt speech: "So you were in Italy?" "Three years, Your Excellency." "Perhaps you also visited the buried places near Naples?" "As a matter of fact, that was the purpose of my trip. I made myself comfortable in an ancient house in Pompeii, and for two years all the excavations took place under my very eyes." "Delighted to hear it, delighted!" exclaimed Goethe, who favoured a compact manner of speaking and liked to leave out the personal pronoun. Moving his chair up to mine, he eagerly continued: "Have repeatedly urged the academies in Vienna and Berlin to send young artists to those subterranean treasures, so that they might study the ancient paintings. So much the better, then, that you did so on your own. Yes, indeed, classical antiquity must be the model for any artist. But let us not forget the best: daresay you have some sketches in your suitcase?" "I usually tried to trace and copy in colour the most beautiful frescoes, as soon as they had been discovered. Would Your Excellency care to see some of them?" "Indeed I would, indeed,"

Goethe interjected, "And thank you! Do come back for lunch. Eat about two o'clock. There will be some other art lovers there. Am really looking forward to your drawings. Good-bye, my young friend." And he firmly shook my hand.

When I returned at the appointed hour, I walked through a number of rooms decorated in the same fashion until I came to the dining room, where I found Goethe and his other guests already assembled: apart from Coudray, von Müller, and Vogel, I saw Riemer, Eckermann, and Meyer. All the guests, as well as Goethe himself, were in formal dress ... I sat between Goethe and Miss Ulrike von Pogwisch, a favourite of the poet's to whom he often addressed himself and to whose replies he listened with obvious pleasure. Facing us sat Ottilie, Ulrike's sister and the poet's daughter-in-law. I found the food exceedingly tasty and the wine at least as good. A bottle of red or white had been placed before each guest. Intending to keep a clear head for what was to follow, I diluted mine with water. Goethe noticed it and rebuked me: "Where did you acquire that bad habit?" The conversation was general, animated, and continuous; Goethe directed it masterfully, without restricting anyone. All about him sat his living encyclopedias on whom he would call on occasion since he did not wish to burden himself with the dead weight of booklearning. Riemer represented philosophy, Meyer art history, and Eckermann turned out to be a veritable storehouse of quotations on any number of subjects; he listened with bated breath to the master's words, which he appeared to commit to memory instantly like so many Delphic oracles ... The table talk revolved especially around Italy and its art treasures; loosing my timid and awkward tongue, Goethe had me report on my studies in the Vatican. They all remembered Rome with delight and greatly praised its splendours. Only Miss Ulrike felt that she had to give vent to her Protestant indignation against the Pope and his government. Smiling, Goethe handed the young zealot a toothpick: "Here, my daughter, revenge yourself with this!" he said good-humouredly, and I wondered whether in handing her this odd weapon, he made allusion to my name [Zahn=tooth]. He had emptied a whole bottle and poured himself a glass from a second one when we were already being given our coffee. Then we got up, tables were pushed together and a white cloth spread on them, and I unfolded and explained my sketches. They liked in particular "Leda with the Nest from which Castor, Pollux, and Helena peek out", "Achilles and Briseis", "Pasithea's and Hypnos' Marriage", "Jupiter Enthroned" and "Bacchus Enthroned"—all coloured sketches, reproduced on tracing paper, of Pompeiian frescoes which had been brought to light from under a thirty-foot layer of ashes. Goethe examined each painting lovingly and remarked on it in the most expert and striking fashion. His comments proved to me how deeply this genius had penetrated into the essence of art and the secrets of the Hellenic mind. Suddenly, firm steps rang out behind us, and when I turned I saw a square-set man in a forage cap and a short hunting jacket of green velvet embroidered in gold braid. It was the Grand Duke . . . who had come in through the garden and back door, to which he always had a key. Goethe welcomed him with the characteristic words: "Your Highness has arrived in time for a feast!" Charles Augustus had a short meerschaum pipe in his hand, from which he was in the habit of puffing continually but which he let go out now since Goethe abhorred tobacco . . .

I had intended to leave Weimar the next day, but Goethe urged me to remain at least another two weeks and to visit him every day. The Grand Duke invited me for lunch the following day, but before I had a chance to reply, Goethe exclaimed: "No, at noon Zahn belongs to me!", and Charles Augustus did not insist. Most of the guests had already departed, except Coudray, Eckermann, and Ottilie. I, too, was about to take my leave when Goethe held me back saying: "Feel like more of your sketches. Will you show them to us?" In the meantime, he had divested himself of his morning coat and exchanged it for a comfortable housecoat. Then he took his place in an armchair while the others stood around it and his grandsons Walther and Wolfgang, who had meanwhile entered, pressed close to him as I interpreted the drawings. He particularly admired "Iphigenia's Sacrifice" and "Hercules finding his Son Telephus suckled by a Hind". Goethe was absorbed in quiet reflection, and finally said: "Yes, the ancients are truly unequalled in every field of

inspired art. You see, gentlemen, I, too, think that I have achieved
something, but compared to one of the great poets of Attica, to
Aeschylus or Sophocles, I am a nobody."[14]

3

The Romantics

'Faut-il s'étonner . . . que les plus sublimes scènes de la création
soient contemplées d'un œil si divers par les voyageurs? C'est
que chacun porte avec soi son point de vue . . . *Le spectacle est
dans le spectateur.*'

LAMARTINE in *Graziella*

ON A SUMMER evening shortly before the July Revolution, Lamartine
found himself a guest at a soirée during which the actor Lafond
declaimed scenes from Chateaubriand's *Moïse*. It was an elegant
occasion, of a kind to which the younger poet, who had spent much
time away from Paris and whose days of mundane splendour were
still to come, was not often invited. The salon was that of Juliette
Récamier's 'Abbaye-aux-Bois' and the guest of honour none other than
the author himself, Juliette's friend the Vicomte de Chateaubriand,
on leave from his duties as French ambassador to the Holy See.
Lamartine has left a description, *méchante* but probably accurate, of
his older and then much more illustrious fellow-poet (who was to even
the account later by referring to the other man, whose name he pre-
tended not to remember, as 'M. de Lamartinière'). Seated under a
portrait of Madame de Staël and looking 'like an aged Oswald',
Chateaubriand was so dissatisfied with the reading that he rose from
his chair, disengaged himself from the circle of admiring ladies which
had formed around him, and took the manuscript out of the hapless
actor's hand in order to declaim the work himself. Even so, it took all
of Madame Récamier's charm, a charm which had tamed men like
Joachim Murat and the Duke of Wellington, to save the occasion; the
drama was so weak that not even the author's own declamation could
make it sound convincing.

It is as good as certain that no one thought of Pompeii that evening.
Yet Madame de Staël, who had died in 1817, had been as fascinated by
the city as were Chateaubriand and Lamartine. Remote as it was from
the glitter of Restoration Paris, the Pompeiian experience can in fact

be said to have formed a bond not only between these disparate writers, but among many representatives of Romanticism as a whole. These men and women tended to record not what they had *seen*, but what they had *felt* on the site. Not that the epistolary accounts suddenly died out; Shelley, for one, was fully as precise in describing what he saw in 1819 as De Brosses had been eighty years before him; but side by side with this topographical treatment which is in essence a picture recorded in letter form, there now appears an interpretative one in which the picture is diffracted through the prism of a personality: an image recorded in a variety of poetic forms. If Pompeii now becomes for many who visited it a 'city of the soul' as Rome was for Byron, this development is interesting not in itself—the transformation of pictures into images is characteristic of all literature—but because of the polarity inherent in the subject. Pompeii is a place in which the thought of *Sic transit* occurs even to the dullest mind; at the same time, it represents one of the most painstakingly investigated localities on earth. This is no haunting ruin on a windswept shore, no pretty hamlet encompassing all domestic virtues, no solitary moor shrouded in Ossianic mists; Pompeii is, and was already in the Romantic period, a city which has been cold-bloodedly excavated stone by stone and measured inch by inch. An evocative spot, to be sure; but also an utterly prosaic one whose history is firmly marked on the network of geographical and cultural co-ordinates of educated men everywhere. Upon this universal network the Romantics now super-imposed that of their individual minds, moods, and memories, and in doing so they added, each in his own way, many characteristic touches not only to Pompeiian but to Romantic literature. It is no wonder that the resultant image was often distorted, and artistically so complex that it could no longer be expressed in a mere letter.

In calling Chateaubriand an 'aged Oswald', much as we might refer to someone as a 'poor man's Hamlet' or a 'would-be Lolita', Lamartine paid a remarkable tribute to the hero of a novel which had been published many years before. It had swept Europe at the time and was discussed not only in literary circles but in the Tuileries, where the Emperor of France is said to have flung the volume into a corner when he detected its anti-French tendency. If the book thus helped to perpetuate a feud famous in history, that between Napoleon and Germaine de Staël, it also served to cement two celebrated romances: that between Shelley and Emilia Viviani, the heroine of *Epipsychidion*, and the even more turbulent one of Byron and Teresa Guiccioli into whose copy of the novel the poet wrote an impassioned declaration of love which ends, somewhat incongruously, with the remark that Madame de Staël had been a friend of his. Shelley admired Dante's rendering of the episode of Paolo and Francesca, and Byron translated it into English; when thinking of Germaine and her book, the two friends may well have remembered the famous line '*Galeotto fu 'l libro e chi lo scrisse*'.—Madame de Staël's novel is not likely to fan the flames of love in our day, or even to be read much any more. Nonetheless, it is a beacon which once guided countless visitors to Italy and to Pompeii.

Part travelogue and part autobiographical novel, *Corinne, ou l'Italie* remains a curious work. It has been called 'the worst great novel ever written', and a book which must strike the modern reader as 'singularly monotonous'[1]; in reading it one is indeed torn between admiration for the writer's gift of observation and resentment at her disregard of the most elementary logic. The novel contains impressions of Italian customs and landscapes, among them an evocation of Pompeii, which belong among the great pages of travel literature. These descriptive pearls, however, are strung upon so fragile a narrative thread that the reader's enjoyment is overshadowed by the fear that it is all going to end in madness or incest or some other dénouement born not of necessity or logic, but of the need to bring into focus a diffuse and most unlikely plot.

Ostensibly and on the first plane, it is the love story of Oswald Lord Nelvil, a suitably dour Scottish peer in his mid-twenties, and the *improvvisatrice* Corinne, a young woman whose skill in the creation of unpremeditated poetry (sung to the accompaniment of a lyre) has made her famous throughout Italy. Oswald, who had travelled to Rome with a vainglorious Frenchman, the Comte d'Erfeuil, and distinguished himself on the way by single-handedly bringing under control a fire which threatened to devastate the city of Ancona, first lays eyes on Corinne when she is being crowned poetess laureate in a public ceremony on the Capitol. He soon makes her acquaintance and falls in love, but all his questions about her background and circumstances remain unanswered. Nor is he at all communicative about his own affairs; taciturn by nature, he is further depressed because he feels unworthy of his father, who had died before he could bless him and forgive him for an act of insubordination. Living only in the present and afraid that their bliss will end the moment they discuss their past, Corinne and Oswald explore together the antiquities, art treasures, folk customs, and society life of Rome, sometimes by themselves and on other occasions with Count d'Erfeuil and Prince Castelforte, an elderly admirer of Corinne's and the man who had placed the laurel wreath, reminiscent of Petrarch and Tasso, on her brow in the Capitol. In their conversations during these sightseeing trips and in the letters by which they communicate at other times, Corinne, who epitomizes all that is lovable and spontaneous in the Italian character, gradually weans Oswald away from his introspectiveness and converts him to what in default of a more precise term might be called the Mediterranean way of life. Yet their relationship, which has meanwhile ripened into passion, brings them no happiness; somehow, they are star-cross'd lovers, although we are not given the reason until they travel to Naples in the second half of the book. It is on the occasion of this trip, after their visit to Pompeii, that Oswald and Corinne realize that they can no longer shut out the past and the future. Their friends look upon them as engaged if not secretly married, and the times are so unsettled, that summer of 1795, that Oswald may be recalled at any moment to his regiment in England. At the Hermitage of San Salvador, half-way up Mount Vesuvius, he finally tells his story, at night while they watch the fiery lava flow down the slopes and light up the valleys beneath them: 'You shall see into the depths of my soul. I will tell you all and reopen my wounds. I feel it is best to do so; in the presence of this unchangeable nature, fear seems natural.'[2]

Oswald, we are told, had been sent to France some years earlier because his father wanted him to see something of the world before taking up the obligations incumbent upon him as a peer's only son: marriage (to Lucilla Edgermond, a neighbouring squire's daughter), the army, Parliament. In Paris, the young man had fallen in love with

Madame d'Arbigny, a widow whose family had died under the guillotine. Having failed to gain his father's permission to marry her, Oswald had stayed on in France beyond the six months agreed upon by the elder Lord Nelvil, in order to protect the lady from the fate of her relatives. He returned to England only when he discovered that she was what in novels of that vintage used to be called 'unworthy of his love'—too late, as it turned out, because his disappointed father had meanwhile died. Haunted by remorse, Oswald then gave himself over to the melancholy of which Corinne had only just cured him.

Apart from his father's disapproval of marriage to a foreigner, there seems to be nothing in Oswald's past to prevent him from sharing his life with Corinne. Her own story, however, still remains to be told, and before doing so she gives a last improvised recitation, after sunset at Cap Miseno, where there lies spread before them 'the whole country from Naples to Gaeta, the land where are left the most numerous of volcanoes, history, and poetry'. Obsessed by the thought that she may lose her lover, Corinne evokes '*les souvenirs que ces lieux retraçaient*': the shades of the women who gave up their love, and life itself, on these very shores. In a final and highly dramatic dirge she mourns the fate of Cornelia, the widow of Pompey, of Agrippina who wept for Germanicus, of Portia taking leave of Brutus. After returning to Naples, Corinne sends Oswald the manuscript in which she has set down the history of her life.

She is the daughter of Lord Edgermond and his first wife, an Italian lady who had died when Corinne was very young. Her father had then returned to Scotland and married the present Lady Edgermond, who also presented him with a daughter: Lucilla, Corinne's half-sister—and Oswald's fiancée. Not unnaturally, Lady Edgermond preferred her own to her step-daughter, who in turn detested the country gentlewoman's life that was in store for her and yearned for the warmth and the colours of her native Italy. She was not badly treated, but her impulsiveness endeared her neither to Lady Edgermond nor to their neighbour, Lord Nelvil, who had long wanted to arrange a marriage between his son Oswald and one of Lord Edgermond's daughters. He had at first thought of Corinne; shocked by her un-English forthrightness, he then changed his mind and decided that when the time came,

9 Ferdinand IV; a bust by Antonio Canova. Museo
Filangeri, Naples.

10 Maria Carolina, painted during her exile in Naples.
Museo della Certosa di S. Martino, Naples.

his son should marry the demure Lucilla instead. In the meantime, however, Lord Edgermond died. Corinne, now a young woman, thereupon returned to Italy, where, independent thanks to her inheritance and admired on account of her poetic gifts, she soon assumed a prominent role in the social and artistic life of Rome. Although Lucilla had been sorry to see her leave, the spiteful Lady Edgermond was so relieved that she gave out the news, back in Scotland, that her stepdaughter had died abroad.

Knowing that Corinne was once intended for him but that his father had considered her ill-suited for the position of a future Lady Nelvil, Oswald now decides to return to Scotland. Giving his ring to Corinne during a tearful farewell scene in Venice, with the promise that he will not get married unless it be to her, he leaves with the resolve to break off his engagement to Lucilla and to compel Lady Edgermond to acknowledge Corinne again as her step-daughter. But once he is back among his own people, he has second thoughts. Not only does the formidable Lady Edgermond turn out to be a frail old lady whose last wish it is to see her daughter suitably married; Lucilla herself has meanwhile developed into an attractive young woman accomplished in all the social, domestic, and equestrian graces expected of someone of her background. The 'right' man, of course, is none other than Oswald himself, who is much taken with Lucilla and gradually convinces himself that his liaison with Corinne was a mere infatuation. Corinne, who has had no news of Oswald because the outbreak of war held up the mails, now senses that she is losing her place in his heart. In a desperate attempt to regain that place, she travels to England herself. From a distance and without making her presence known to them, she observes Oswald and Lucilla at public ceremonies, such as a march-past in Hyde Park, and in society. Concluding that the two are made for each other, she determines to stand aside and to release her lover from his promise. She accordingly sends back his ring and, despairing of ever finding happiness again, returns to Italy alone. As soon as Oswald finds out that she had actually followed him to his homeland, he is smitten by remorse at his callousness; by then, however, he is married and soon to be a father. The war with France having meanwhile begun in earnest, years pass before he is able to come to Italy and beg Corinne's

7

forgiveness for not having remained true to her and to all that was best in himself also. When he does see her again, with his wife and little daughter, it is too late. Corinne, broken in spirit and with her poetic vein silenced forever, can forgive him only on her deathbed.

It is clear even from this cursory sketch that *Corinne* is among other things a veritable school-book example of a Romantic novel. Its genuineness in this regard, from the largely epistolary form to the posing and resolution of the theme itself, surely contributed to its success in its own time and to the relative oblivion to which it has since been consigned (in contrast to less flamboyant works of the period, including Madame de Staël's own *De l'Allemagne*). On another and nowadays perhaps more meaningful level, *Corinne* is a biographical and autobiographical work from which literary historians have been able to illuminate many details in Germaine de Staël's life which might otherwise have remained obscure. Beyond this they have traced, ever since the days of the Schlegel brothers and Sainte-Beuve, certain parallels between the men and women who appear in the novel and the real-life individuals who may have lent them some trait or other of their own personality and fate. These detective labours have been so generously rewarded that they have provided us with an entertaining Who's Who of the literary figures and the *beau monde* of the early nineteenth century.

In the figure of Oswald, for example, elements of several persons belonging to Germaine's entourage have been discovered: of Louis de Narbonne-Lara, Benjamin Constant, Dom Pedro de Souza, Prosper de Barante, and Maurice O'Donnell, as well as of the historian Edward Gibbon (who once had to be dissuaded by *his* father from marrying a foreigner: Suzanne Curchod, who eventually became Madame Necker and Germaine's mother) and even of Lord Nelson, whose triumphal reception by the Italians, as their protector against Napoleon, may have found a reflection in Oswald's popularity with the good people of Ancona; indeed, the very name Nelvil is sometimes thought to have been derived from Nelson. Similarly, Prince Castelforte may be a composite of Mathieu de Montmorency-Laval and of no fewer than three poets: August Wilhelm von Schlegel, Vincenzo Monti, and that Giuseppe Alborghetti who had recited passages from Madame de

Staël's works when the authoress was being received into the Academy. In Count d'Erfeuil, the archetype of the foppish Frenchman which so enraged Napoleon, one has recognized young Claude Hochet, and in Madame d'Arbigny the Comtesse de Flahaut, mother of Talleyrand's illegitimate son. By such tokens and for what they may be worth, the figure of Corinne herself has reminded scholars of Pauline de Beaumont, Chateaubriand's 'Dilecta', who had travelled to Rome expressly in order to die in his arms (and in recognition was given a splendid marble tomb built with funds partially supplied by Delphine de Custine, her successor in those arms); of Angelica Kauffmann, beloved of Joshua Reynolds and admired by Goethe; of the ubiquitous Juliette Récamier; and above all of Emma Hamilton, like Corinne an English-woman more appreciated in Italy than at home, the companion of a celebrated English visitor to southern shores, and a woman whose means of artistic expression—in Emma's case, the acting out, pictur-esquely draped and occasionally be-turbaned à la Madame de Staël, of the famous 'attitudes'—did not seem to fit into the more traditional patterns of terpsichorean or literary achievement.

But more than anyone else, Corinne is Germaine de Staël herself, whose journey of 1804-5 took her to Pompeii and the other localities described in the novel, the action of which is set ten years earlier. It is the writer, as much as her heroine, who represents the woman of genius chained to love's chariot, and if Prince Castelforte asks: 'And your friends, Corinne—your friends! Where will you be loved as here?' the remark must have come straight from the heart of Madame de Staël who had been fêted in Italy like no other woman before her. If not exactly crowned Poetess Laureate, she had at least been made a *pastourelle* of the same Accademia dell'Arcadia (Académie de Rome in the book) which had already welcomed to its ranks Queen Christina of Sweden and Goethe. It was, in fact, on the occasion of this reception, on February 14, 1805, that she first laid eyes on *her* Oswald: Dom Pedro de Souza e Holstein, a Portuguese duke who despite his name was no relation of her husband's, but disturbingly handsome and a good deal younger than herself. They met again the same evening, in the house of the Prussian ambassador to the Holy See, Wilhelm von Humboldt, and no doubt experienced in each other's company many of the events described as having been witnessed by the fictional lovers. While it is true that she was not an *improvvisatrice* like Corinne, the Sibylline aspect was strong in Germaine also. She was often called a prophetess, and is so portrayed in Madame Vigée-Lebrun's famous portrait. Historians of literature have thus identified with their real-life models many persons and motifs found in *Corinne*. Before we consider the central place which the Pompeiian episode occupies in the novel as its half-way mark, its epic turning point, and its emotional point of no return, a few words are in order about the idea which Madame de Staël's generation had formed of Italy as a whole.

Foremost among the peculiarities of eighteenth- and early nineteenth-century visitors to Italy was a predilection for localities which the modern tourist would consider as out-of-the-way and of secondary importance. The traveller with cultural interests (businessmen, actors, the clergy, and others whose journey is primarily determined by professional considerations have their own itineraries) will usually endeavour to 'do' first of all the great art centres. If at all limited in time, money, and sightseeing stamina, he will tend to devote his first and in many cases his only trip to the 'habitation of departed greatness', to Rome, Naples, Florence, and Venice, and perhaps to this or that region of particular appeal such as the Tuscan and Umbrian hill-towns, Sicily, or the lake country North of Milan. He is not likely to follow Wordsworth's example in visiting Milan and Vallombrosa rather than Rome and Naples; neither will he settle in Rome, in the manner of Keats, without also looking at Florence and Venice, or, like Shelley, forego Sicily for the Ligurian coast. These shifts of accentuation are due not only to changing fashion, but to a number of eminently practical considerations. If some cities of relatively slight artistic appeal such as Turin, Leghorn, or Genoa drew forth raptures of delight from travellers who had yet to see Venice and Naples, it is because they happen to lie on the route taken by the French and English who entered the country through the western Alps. For the same reason, Germans and Scandinavians who came over the Brenner were wont to spend what would now be considered an unconscionably long time in towns like Peschiera and Modena. Goethe's praise of Lake Garda,

Stendhal's lifelong attachment to Milan, Lamartine's interest in Leghorn, and Shelley's plan of spending his first Italian winter on Lake Como (which his wife Mary sensibly dissuaded him from carrying out) did not spring from some obscure personal foible on the part of these men, but from the joy of having finally arrived in the country of their dreams, from relief at having safely crossed the Alps, and in many cases also from the need to recuperate from the rigours of that crossing. Such factors do not apply to the modern traveller who often arrives by plane or ship, and even if he drives or takes the train is spared the hardships suffered by Winckelmann, who spent a day covering two miles near the Brenner Pass, or Walpole, who thought his last hour had come when a wolf carried off, near Mont Cenis, his favourite dog which had been trotting by his side.

Other localities owed their reputation to strategic factors which no longer apply. If Ancona is so prominently mentioned in the literature of the time, it is because the city was an apple of discord in Napoleon's and Nelson's struggle for supremacy in the Mediterranean. In similar fashion the little town of Terracina, also described in *Corinne*, was then looked upon as one of the most dangerous spots in all Italy. Surrounded on three sides by mountains and lying on the border between the badly administered Kingdom of the Two Sicilies and the equally ill-governed Papal States, it was infested by bandits. In 1811, Lamartine witnessed a robbery there which could have held its own in any Hollywood Western: a stagecoach in flames, two passengers and a wounded horse stretched out on the road, the Naples Constabulary riding up in the manner of the 7th U.S. Cavalry. It was in Terracina, and not in Rome, Milan, or Paris as one might expect, that Stendhal first met Rossini in 1817. Washington Irving later celebrated the town in *The Inn at Terracina*, and in the 1840's Alfred de Musset could still playfully ask his brother, in the little poem by which he welcomed him back from Italy:

> 'Les brigands t'ont-ils arrêté
> Sur le chemin tant redouté
> De Terracine . . . ?'

Terracina, alas! has long ago ceased to be *redouté*; it is no more now than it was in ancient times, a minor port between Anzio and Gaeta.

Still other cities, finally, were considered desirable for reasons entirely unconnected with their geographic or cultural importance. So many English poets had come to settle in Pisa, for example, that Mary Shelley could describe the city in 1821 as 'a little nest of singing birds'; yet there is no evidence that the two nightingales among them, Byron and Shelley, ever looked at the famous frescoes in the Campo Santo. Florence, too, acted as a powerful magnet on a whole generation, not of young artists who wanted to study in the Uffizi but of middle-aged French tourists who came to pay their respects to three portly gentlemen with innocuous-sounding names—the Counts of Saint-Leu and Survilliers, and the Prince of Montfort—who were spending a few years of carefree exile on the banks of the Arno in the 1820s and 30s. They were Napoleon's brothers, and had once been kings: Louis Bonaparte of Holland, Joseph of Naples and Spain, and Jérôme of Westphalia.

It is against this background that we must gauge the prominence given to Pompeii in *Corinne*. By 1807, when this novel which itself set a fashion was first published, the Campanian cities had become fashionable stops on the Grand Tour. They were at least as fashionable as Venice, which despite its beauty and history, and the delightful aura of wickedness which had enveloped it during the last decades of its political independence, comes off rather badly in the novel. Rousseau and Winckelmann had written on Venice, and their marked lack of enthusiasm had no doubt affected many lesser spirits. The 'Sun-girt City's' great days in literature, the days of Shelley, Byron, De Musset and George Sand, Platen, Ruskin, Nietzsche, Wagner, Hofmannsthal, and Thomas Mann were still, so to speak, just around the corner.

If the classification of the most desirable Italian localities thus differed from that presently in force, the order in which the country's great men presented themselves to the Romantics was equally at variance with ours. Few would hesitate nowadays to name Dante, Petrarch, and Boccaccio as the outstanding writers of older Italian letters, and Michelangelo, Leonardo, and Raphael as the most distinguished Renaissance artists. It is, in part, the very eminence of these men which draws us to Rome and Florence, and elsewhere to such specific sites as Dante's abode in Verona or Leonardo's 'Last Supper' in Milan. Yet Leonardo is barely mentioned among the numerous painters whose work is discussed in *Corinne*. Madame de Staël seems to have thought as little of him as Shelley did of Michelangelo, or Byron of Petrarch. One could easily draw up a list of such entertaining misconceptions treasured by the Romantics, from Stendhal's reference to Monti as 'the greatest living poet' to Shelley's conviction that Theodosius rather than Theoderic lies buried in Ravenna. But in the final instance, such short-circuits are irrelevant to the achievement of these poets; they are important only insofar as they indicate that many literary and aesthetic notions treasured by the Romantics—some of whom still preferred a painter like Guido Reni, the 'divine Guido', to Titian—had more in common with those of preceding generations than with our own.

Already in the eighteenth century there had developed, in France with Volney and Diderot and in England with Dyer and Turnbull, a school of poets who revelled in the melancholy engendered by the aspect of ruins and in those '*méditations sur les révolutions des empires*' which form the core of Volney's *Les ruines*. The theme was taken up by Robert, Fragonard, Clérisseau, and other *peintres de ruines*, and a walk around the Coliseum,

> 'When the rising moon begins to climb
> Its topmost arch, and gently pauses there;
> When the stars twinkle through the loops of time,
> And the low night-breeze waves along the air
> The garland forest . . .'

had become the high point of many a visit to the Eternal City even before Byron wrote *Childe Harold*. (Corinne, too, undertakes this pilgrimage, and on the proper occasion: on the eve of her departure from Rome.) Even so, it was not enough for a building to be old and in a state of disrepair in order to be celebrated in song; it also had to be non-functional. Although they often reached further back in time than the Coliseum or the Pompeiian Forum, the roads, aqueducts, and bridges of antiquity were neglected in favour of less utilitarian ruins such as tombs and temples. The word *tombeau* occurs in two separate chapter headings in *Corinne*, and the relatively 'modern' tombs of

Dante in Ravenna, of Petrarch at Arquâ, and of Tasso in Rome were fully as popular as were those along the Via Appia Antica, or the Via dei Sepolcri in Pompeii. The most famous tomb of all, appropriately enough, was that of Virgil, on the Posillipo in Naples. The laurel bush which shaded this pyramidal brick structure was gradually being despoiled by visitors who broke off, and frequently sent home to friends, a twig emblematic of valour and fame. Stimulated by visitors returning from Rome, Pompeii, and Paestum, the temple craze had exacted its tribute somewhat earlier, in the form of such imitations as the Temple de Vesta at Méréville and the Temple de l'Amour in the park at Trianon.

Not only buildings and monuments, but entire landscapes had become the goal of sentimental pilgrimages. One such site was Pompeii, then so treasured on account of the nostalgic mood it inspired that its didactic function, as the source of much of our information about the domestic life of the ancients, was often altogether overlooked; another was the Roman *campagna*, hitherto only appreciated by the painters Lorrain and Poussin. Many literary men had traversed this malaria-ridden region, from Montaigne and Milton to Walpole and Winckelmann, and they seem to have disliked it as much as De Brosses, who suspected that Romulus must have been drunk when he obeyed the dream which had bidden him found a city 'in so ugly a region'.[3] Although Chateaubriand and C.-V. de Bonstetten had struck a new chord soon to be echoed in *Corinne* and amplified by Stendhal, George Sand could still write, decades later in *La Daniella*, that the *agro romano* was '*laid, trois fois laid et stupide*'.[4] These and similar predilections were part of the Romantic quest of the past, and in the final instance, of the abstracted past, of memory itself. Chateaubriand's belief that a place is worth only as much as the memories one takes away from it—*un site ne vaut que par les souvenirs*—is taken up by many of his contemporaries and reiterated by Madame de Staël in Pompeii.

The Romantic mind is of course too complex a phenomenon to be explained within so idiosyncratic a frame of reference; but enough has been said to indicate the extent to which these predilections have found expression in *Corinne*. The novel's seminal role in later travel literature is, however, enhanced by other factors as well: by Germaine's eminence

among the writers of her time; by the date of publication, when
Romanticism had just burst into bloom in England (within a year of
the French original, two translations had been published across the
Channel) and was fermenting powerfully in France and Germany; and
by the fact that the author had visited Italy in such select company.
August Wilhelm von Schlegel, her mentor and guide and the tutor of
her children, lives on in the history of literature as a great critic and
translator. Germaine herself regarded him somewhat more coolly, as a
fine scholar whose lack of social *désinvolture* also made him a bit of a
bore. She was a compulsive talker of strongly didactic inclinations, and
as a result of her censure the poor man came to believe himself at times
altogether unworthy of membership in the exalted circle which she had
assembled at Coppet and on her peregrinations throughout Europe.
Unlike Goethe, who was merely amused and impressed when he met
her on her tour of Germany, Schlegel had let himself be swept along
in her wake and suddenly found himself transported from the libraries
and museums of provincial Berlin into the limelight of mundane
belles-lettres. So total, in fact, had been his subjugation that at the time
of their Pompeiian interlude, he was less than a year away from signing
his Articles of Surrender, that extraordinary document which begins
with the statement 'I declare that you have every right over me and
that I have none over you . . .'

Although it is unlikely that Germaine was in love with Schlegel or
with her other travelling companion, Simonde de Sismondi, the author
of a celebrated *Histoire des républiques italiennes du moyen âge*, she owed
much to these men. Having an ear for Italian music and for the
language but little knowledge of the country's history and art, she
perceived the latter through the medium of Sismondi's enthusiasm and
Schlegel's erudition. Precisely because she had the benefit of such
expert guidance, her attitude to Italy as a whole is typical of that held
by the best of her generation. Neither her relative indifference to
Florence nor her discovery of the 'good' people of Naples (and of the
'evil' Bourbon rule under which they 'chafed'); neither her admiration
of the Pantheon and Coliseum nor her neglect of other Roman attractions (for example, of the fountains which are so popular in our own
days); neither her words on Canova nor her silence on Leonardo set

her apart from the majority of her contemporaries. A case in point is
the reference to Goethe, which had come to be expected of the well-
bred early nineteenth-century traveller to Italy. If she pays tribute to
Der Fischer and *Römischer Karneval* in her novel, her compatriot
Lamartine does no less in quoting *Kennst du das Land* in *Graziella*, and
Gautier, *Sarkophagen und Urnen* in *Arria Marcella*.

One is the more surprised, then, to discover a specific and truly
Staëlian tone in her description of Pompeii,

'the most curious ruins of antiquity. In Rome you simply find relics
of antiquity, and in these you just trace the political history of past
ages; but at Pompeii the private life of the ancients offers itself to
your reflection. The volcano which covered this city with cinders
has preserved it from the ravages of time. If the buildings had been
exposed to the air, they would have decayed, but this buried remembrance is perfectly preserved. Pictures and bronzes have all their
first beauty, and vessels of domestic use are in entire preservation.
The amphoras stand ready for the coming feast, and the corn which
was being ground is there. The remains of a lady, still ornamented
with the decorations she wore on the day the volcano interrupted the
feast, are seen, with her dried arms filling no longer the bracelets of
precious stones which encircle them—you realize how this figure
was struck down in the midst of life. Red furrows seam the pavements in the streets, and the wall stones carry traces of what little by
little has hollowed them. On the walls of a rampart are some coarsely
traced figures that the sentinels had cut for pastime, just before they
were engulfed. In one place four streets meet, and from this spot you
can see the whole town. You are surrounded by objects of life in the
days gone by, and their eternal silence seems all the more sad. There
are some pieces of petrified lava broken off, which have been again
covered with another flood. So ruin upon ruin, tomb upon tomb!
This history of the world, of which the epochs are counted by ruins,
and this human life, the trace of which is only seen by the light of
the volcanoes which have destroyed it, fill our hearts with profound
melancholy. Here, for a long time, man lived, loved, suffered, and
then perished—but where will you find his feelings, his thoughts?
A few leaves of scorched mss., found at Herculaneum and Pompeii,

and which they have essayed to decipher at Portici, are all we have to tell us of the unhappy victims which the volcano, that earth lightning, had devoured. While you pass these cinders, which seem almost to breathe, you scarcely tread for fear some power should raise this dust, where noble ideas once reigned.

The public buildings in the town of Pompeii, though the least imposing in Italy, are still beautiful. The luxury of the ancients had always for its mark objects of public interest. Their houses were particularly small, and showed less a rare or magnificent taste than a love of the fine arts, since their interiors are ornamented by very pretty paintings, and the floors are of artistic mosaic. On some of the pavements is written the word "*Salve*"; it is also put on the lintel of the door, and not only means courtesy, but also hospitality. The rooms were narrow and ill-lighted, the windows never opening into the street, but to a portico in the interior, surrounding a marble court, in the centre of which is a reservoir simply decorated. It is evident, from the whole arrangement, that the inhabitants lived out of doors, and also received their friends there. Nothing gives a sweeter or more voluptuous idea of life than a climate which intimately unites man to nature. You can entertain in a much more lively way in these regions, than when extreme cold obliges you to shut yourself and your friends in a house. You can better comprehend Plato's dialogues when you see the porticoes under which the ancients promenaded half the day. They were unceasingly animated by a beautiful sky, and their social order was not a dry combination of calculation and force, but a happy union of institutions, which exercised the faculties, developed the soul, and gave to man for an incentive his own and his fellows' perfection. Antiquity inspires an insatiable curiosity. Scholars, who occupy themselves by merely getting together a succession of names and calling it history, are surely devoid of imagination; but to penetrate the past; to interrogate the human heart across the ages; to seize a fact by a word, and the character and manners of a nation by a fact; to go back to remote times, and to judge by the few remains how the earth appeared to man in his youth, and how man sustained the gift of life, and what civilization has accomplished meanwhile—this is a continual effort to the imagination, as it tries to discover the delightful secrets that reflection and study can reveal to us. This sort of interest and occupation singularly attracted Oswald, and he often told Corinne that if he had not the noble duty of serving his native land to perform, he would only find life supportable in a country where the monuments of history take the place of present existence; he felt it at least necessary to regret glory if it were not possible to obtain it. It is forgetfulness alone that can degrade a soul, for if cruel circumstances remove all sources of present joy, it can find an asylum in the past.'

In these sentences, the smooth contours of a romanticized Italy are broken up by features which transcend both the traditional Pompeiian reflexes—the reference to the uniqueness of the locale ('the most curious ruins of antiquity'), the awareness of time-arrested-in-its-tracks ('the corn which was being ground') and of life cruelly snuffed out ('her dried arms filling no longer . . .')—and their specifically Romantic variants such as the contrast with other cities ('in Rome . . . but at Pompeii') or the emphasis on emotional density rather than descriptive detail ('silence . . . sad . . . ruin upon ruin, tomb upon tomb . . . profound melancholy', but not one building, street, or art object mentioned by name). The passage even transcends that larger Italian network of co-ordinates which Schlegel and Sismondi had designed for their pupil. One is reminded of a younger Germaine, of the girl who had conversed in her mother's salon with Diderot, d'Alembert, and Voltaire, and of the young woman who had written *Lettres sur Jean-Jacques Rousseau*. Although the fictional Corinne is the very model of a Romantic *innamorata*, she disappears from view here, with her lover by her side and a few hours before her fate is to be decided, and is replaced by the living Madame de Staël who reacts to the scene as an eighteenth-century moralist for whom the ethical function of art outweighs the sensual pleasures afforded by its contemplation. The *means* by which she travels into the past are those of 1805: an evocative re-creation of history rather than an enumeration of the men and events which have shaped its course; indeed, she clearly dissociates herself from those who would prefer 'getting together a succession of names and calling it history'. But her *destination* is that of an earlier and strongly rationalistic period, almost as if she were on a voyage into her own past: a survey of this particular civilization in terms of its laws and institutions, and—shades of Montesquieu!—even of its physical and climatic setting. This Pompeiian civilization, in turn, is viewed not as an object in itself but as an index of where its creators, the Romans of the late Republic and early Empire, had stood in relation to man's progress along the spiral of human perfectibility. Schlegel, who had walked through the ruins with Germaine and dragged her through half the museums of Italy while lecturing on art history, is as far away as Sismondi, who was fond of stressing the specifically Italian aspects of whatever scene happened to present itself to the three travellers. There is nothing erudite in this passage, as there is for example in the review which Schlegel was to write of *Corinne*, with its mention of Winckelmann, Goethe, Heinse, and Moritz. There is no reference to the earthquake of 63 or to Pliny, no quotation from Greek or Latin authors (although the novel as a whole has its share of such references), and no hint that the authoress ever felt the temptation, to which many greater writers succumbed, to list the objects found on the site. Nor is there anything 'Italian' in this account, such as a comment on the manner in which the excavations were being carried out or a joke about King Ferdinand (although Germaine loved to gossip and had been presented at court). The only person named is Plato, who had nothing whatever to do with Pompeii and yet belongs there if one looks at the city through Madame de Staël's eyes.

This is not the only instance in *Corinne* in which the heroine has been displaced by her creator; but it is the longest and most important of the passages in which the latter speaks from the deepest layer of her own individuality, as an *encyclopédiste* for whom Pompeii was not a beautiful spot or a romantic ruin or an archeological site or a tourist attraction, but, like the Roman Forum itself, '*une preuve frappante de la grandeur morale de l'homme*'.

It is curious that the city's spectacular natural setting should have failed to inspire François René de Chateaubriand, whose North-American, Levantine, Spanish, and Roman scenes establish him as perhaps the greatest landscape artist in French prose. It is the more curious as he also wrote, at the time of his first visit to the excavations, a hauntingly evocative description of his ascent of Mount Vesuvius, in which one fairly hears the wind howl in the solitary crater while all else is silence, 'that absolute silence which I had felt in the forests of America, at noon, when, holding my breath, I heard only the blood rushing through my temples and the pounding of my heart'.[5] But although the poet is silent on Pompeii, the man Chateaubriand speaks all the more clearly.

Here as elsewhere in his writings, he is disdainful of mere detail and at times even of consistency. He claims to have been shown 'a butcher's or a baker's shop, I forget which', although the presence of a flour mill identified the premises clearly enough; in the graffiti, he sees only 'some mis-spelt . . . Latin words scrawled on the walls'; and his suggestion made in 1804, that everything be left in place and the site itself converted into a museum, is later dismissed, in an account of the excavations as they appeared in 1817, as an *idée spécieuse* advanced by *quelques personnes*. This scion of the old Breton nobility, newly famous in 1804 as author of the *Génie du christianisme* and as Secretary of the French embassy in Rome, is equally scornful of the men who guided him through the ruins. Even when briefly retelling the history of the excavations he mentions not Alcubierre, Winckelmann, or La Vega, but only a faceless *on*—'*on m'a fait remarquer*', '*ce que l'on fait aujour-d'hui*'—reminiscent of the depersonalized 'they' which Walpole had used on the identical occasion. His disdain extends even to the *ciceroni*, the poor devils who make their living by showing visitors around. With Chateaubriand there begins that stream of complaints about the covetousness, prurience, and mendacity of Pompeiian and Vesuvian guides which forms an integral part of Italian travel literature and was not reversed until our own days, when Roger Peyrefitte put himself in the place of a guide who unburdens himself of all the resentments which generations of *ciceroni* had built up against ignorant and frequently tightfisted tourists.[6]

For all his lordly indifference to others, Chateaubriand does quote from the French archaeologist Charles François Mazois, and in fact intimates that the rediscovery of Pompeii and Herculaneum had been due to French initiative from the very beginning. At one point, he flatly and foolishly states that the city walls, the Street of Tombs, the amphitheatre, and the forum had all been cleared during the French occupation of 1806–15. But the patriot was also every inch a royalist, and the French savants who in his view single-handedly restored the cities to the sun had, of course, been minions of Napoleon's family. They had been employed by Joseph, the Emperor's older brother, and by Joachim Murat and his wife Caroline, Napoleon's sister. No one, in fact, was more compromised than Mazois himself, Murat's court painter and the beneficiary of much Bonapartist largesse. Chateaubriand, the professional diplomat, proved equal to the challenge posed by this awkward set of circumstances; by not mentioning Murat and merely referring to him as a ruler 'who had emerged from the ranks of the French army' (even while elsewhere awarding the palm of archaeological achievement to his compatriots), he claims a full measure of *gloire* for France without giving any credit to the Corsican monster. So strong were the poet's Bourbon sympathies that he asserted, alone among his contemporaries, that the excavations launched by Ferdinand and Maria Carolina had been carried out 'very systematically, with the praiseworthy intention of uncovering the city rather than seeking hidden treasure'. It is no coincidence that the person to whom Chateaubriand later addressed the most celebrated comment of his public career—'*Madame, votre fils est mon roi*'—should have been Ferdinand's daughter, the Duchess of Berry.

If such is the tenor of the poet's remarks on Pompeii, what can be said of their value? From the scholarly point of view, very little. His observations are highly idiosyncratic, and the drily descriptive form in which they are couched renders their factual inaccuracies all the more apparent. It is, for example, very unlikely that the occurrence of Pompeii and Herculaneum on the Peutinger Chart can be taken as an indication of the cities' continued habitation after 79, because this medieval map is based on Roman military sketches of doubtful chronological reliability. At the same time, it would be unwise to read into Chateaubriand's passages on Pompeii more than is in them; they do no more than confirm what is otherwise known about their author. More important than his ignorance of the finer points of Pompeiian lore is his enthusiasm for the city itself, and we must not take leave of this author without giving him credit for his many aphorisms on the subject, such as 'Rome is only a vast museum, but Pompeii is antiquity come to life'.

If Madame de Staël looked upon Pompeii *en philosophe* and Chateaubriand *en patriote*, Alphonse de Lamartine may be said to have seen it *en amant*. His first visits to Italy had awakened in him an enduring interest in the buried cities; in later years, it was kept alive by a clay lamp purchased in Pompeii, in that winter of 1811-12 when he had fallen in love with the model of *Graziella*:

> *'Salut, de mes travaux compagne solitaire;*
> *Cher témoin autrefois des plus chères amours!*
> *J'ai perdu mon bonheur, tu gardes ta lumière:*
> *Elle est pure et belle toujours.'*
>
> (*A ma lampe*)

The chief literary result of this journey, undertaken as a consequence of a youthful love affair to which his parents put an end by separating him from the object of his affection, was the little novel *Graziella*, written during a subsequent sojourn on Ischia in 1843-4 and eventually absorbed into the autobiographical *Confidences*. It is the story of an eighteen-year-old Frenchman of good family—the author—who spends a winter in Naples with a friend and goes native by working for a fisherman. During a storm, their little boat is thrown ashore on Procida where Andrea, the fisherman, owns a hut in which he has left his womenfolk. Among these is his daughter Graziella, for whom the author soon develops an affection closer to adolescent camaraderie than to love. When the storm is over and a new boat has been procured, they all cross over to Naples. The other young Frenchman, Lamartine's real-life friend Aymon de Virieu, now returns to France; the author, alone in the strange city and almost penniless, falls ill and might have died if Andrea's family, and especially Graziella, had not looked after him. Touched by this solicitude, he accepts an invitation to move into their house in the Mergellina district. There he spends the winter helping Andrea mend nets and teaching Graziella to read and write. The idyll is shattered when her family decides one day that she should marry Cecco, an earnest and shy cousin who had long courted her. The

Lady Hamilton painted by George Romney. National
allery, London.

12 The death mask of Giacomo Leopardi. Biblioteca Governativa, Cremona.

author, feeling *de trop* in the midst of this family crisis and suddenly
realizing that his own feelings for Graziella have grown into love,
leaves the house for a while; distraught by conflicting emotions, he
aimlessly wanders about Vesuvius and Pompeii. When he returns, the
girl is gone; aghast at the thought of being married to Cecco, she has
run away from home. Suspecting that she went to the hut on Procida
where he first met her, he follows her and arrives just in time: she is
about to enter a convent and has already cut off her hair. She is taken
back to Naples, where her family now promise that they will not force
her to marry Cecco. Graziella, of course, is in love with the author
himself, and he with her; however, they are young and very naïve, and
differences in education and social standing preclude any possibility of
marriage between the French gentleman and the fisherman's daughter
from Procida. They have barely settled down again when Virieu arrives
with a summons for his friend to come back to his family in France.
Like Oswald, the author leaves behind his beloved and promises to
return to her; like Corinne, Graziella dies of a broken heart, while the
faithless lover is condemned to everlasting remorse.

If the novel's autobiographical antecedents are somewhat obscure
(it is not quite certain whether or not the fictional heroine was based on
an actual person), its literary antecedents are easily established. It
stands in the direct line of descent from Bernardin de Saint-Pierre's
Paul et Virginie and Madame de Staël's *Corinne* and is indebted as well
to Rousseau ('More contact and spiritual kinship develops in a week
among men in nature than in ten years among men in society') and to
Goethe's *Werther* ('Man, that pitiful insect which sings a few days
before God of its youth and its loves, and then falls silent forever').[7]
There are passages in *Graziella* which bring to mind Chateaubriand's
Atala and Constant's *Adolphe*, and others which lead further afield.
Among the more predictable motifs is that of Pompeii, a *tombeau* full
of the dust of men which expresses so powerfully the vanity of the
world that the visitor is 'rebounded', as it were, into the arms not of the
loved one, who is far away, but of Love itself, the great rival of Death.
Any detailed description of the site would detract from the cathartic
function which is here imputed to it; indeed, Lamartine's remark 'I
looked at everything, and saw nothing' could occur equally well in

8

other Romantic works in which the Pompeiian motif has been similarly used: in Mérimée's *Lettres à une inconnue*, for example, or Stifter's *Brigitta*.—Implicit in Lamartine's work is another aspect which, while characteristic of many stories set in Italy, now tends to be increasingly connected with Naples and its environs. Gradually and almost imperceptibly, the life of the senses which foreigners had once found in the most diverse parts of the country came to be localized in that region. Gray had discovered Florence to be 'an excellent place to employ all one's animal sensations in'; Goethe had sung the sensual as well as artistic praises of the capital in the *Römische Elegien;* Landor and even Wordsworth had felt the erotic lure of Italy in Como, of all places, where

> 'Slow glides the sail along th' illumin'd shore
> And steals into the shade the lazy oar;
> Soft bosoms breathe around contagious sighs,
> And amorous music on the water dies.'
> (*Descriptive Sketches*)

In writing *Graziella* and in elsewhere calling Italy the *patrie de l'amour* and *pays de la pure et brutale volupté*,[8] Lamartine underlines a motif which we shall find elaborated in the works of some later and lesser Romanticists for whom Pompeii was the locale not only of love and death, but of lust and horror.

The welcome which Madame de Staël, Chateaubriand, and Lamartine found in Italy epitomized, in a manner of speaking, the completion of that French conquest of the peninsula which Napoleon's armies had initiated on the battlefield. Not that these writers, staunch anti-Bonapartists all, saw it in this light; yet the attraction which France had long exerted on the intellectual and artistic life of its neighbour was immeasurably enhanced by the victory of the Revolution at home and of French arms abroad. We are at the beginning of the Italian Risorgimento, and of all the forces which nourished that movement, the cry of *Liberté*, *Égalité*, *Fraternité* which had rung across the Alps in Lamartine's youth proved to be the most potent (last but not least because its later perversion at the hands of Napoleon was less resented in Italy, from whose soil his ancestors had sprung and to

which many members of his family were to be consigned, than in the
other countries of Europe). It is therefore entirely proper that
Lamartine has his alter ego in the novel read not only Tacitus, Tasso,
Bernardin de Saint-Pierre and Madame de Staël, but Foscolo's *Lettere
di Jacopo Ortis*, in which 'a young Italian's passionate desire for the
freedom of his country goes hand in hand with his passion for a
beautiful Venetian lady'. The formulation is Lamartine's, and it could
have been Byron's; the sentiment, at any rate, was universal.

Every tremor emanating from Paris from July 14, 1789 onwards was
registered with especial anxiety in Naples, where the opposing forces
had polarized more sharply than elsewhere in Italy. Rightly or wrongly,
the Neapolitan Liberals felt that their country had suffered more under
the Bourbons than Tuscany had under its Hapsburg Grand Dukes or
Piedmont under the Savoyard Kings, and their partisan ardour increased in measure as the centuries-old dream of a free and united Italy
came to be identified with the cause of revolutionary France. The
Royalists, on the other hand, rallied to the defence not only of their
beloved 'Nasone' but of their Queen, the sister of the martyred Marie
Antoinette. Sir John Acton, the French-born English baronet who
became a Tuscan admiral and, eventually, Prime Minister of the Two
Sicilies, counselled prudence, but Maria Carolina would have none of
it. Repression became so severe that two men who had been seen walking on a street in Naples without the customary pigtail, were suspected
of republican sympathies and thrown in prison. The eruption of
Vesuvius in May 1794 was widely regarded as an expression of divine
wrath over the execution of Louis XVI and Marie Antoinette, and the
golden statue of the city's patron saint, San Gennaro, was once again
carried, by barefooted penitents who had roped themselves together,
to the Maddalena Bridge and there set down with its face turned
toward the mountain, which was thereby commanded to be still.

Although some squadrons of Neapolitan cavalry had fought with the
Austrian army which Napolean defeated during his brillant campaign
of 1796, the Kingdom of the Two Sicilies itself was not much affected
by the conditions of the subsequent Peace of Campo Formio. Em-
boldened by their impunity and by Nelson's presence in Italian waters,
the Neapolitans took it into their heads to invade the Papal States in

1798, when Napoleon had sailed for Egypt and the French had
suffered a series of humiliating defeats along the Rhine and in the
plains of Lombardy. For a few intoxicating days that December, the
lazzarone King occupied the city from which the Caesars had ruled
the world; but the French under Championnet quickly counter-
attacked, retook Rome, and entered Naples so speedily that the royal
family had to be evacuated by Nelson himself, with the aid of Emma
Hamilton who had her servants carry the crown jewels of Naples aboard
H.M.S. Foudroyant before the flagship weighed anchor for Sicily

In Naples, Championnet proceeded to establish the short-lived
Parthenopean Republic, governed by local Jacobins and precariously
supported by the French army. It claimed suzerainty over the penin-
sular portion of the former kingdom while Ferdinand and Maria
Carolina, ensconced in Palermo and protected by the British navy
patrolling the Strait of Messina, ruled on the island. In the following
year they managed to reconquer the mainland portion of the realm
with the aid of Nelson, after Aboukir more than ever master of the
Mediterranean, and of Cardinal Ruffo, who swept upwards from
Calabria with an army of irregulars, brigands, and other *Sanfedisti*
The French and their republican allies soon found themselves restric-
ted to Naples proper, which they were able to evacuate only through
enlisting the help of San Gennaro. (Preserved in two glass vials ever
since he was beheaded in the year 305, the saint's blood traditionally
liquefies in May and September. Had it failed to do so on May 4 1799,
the *lazzaroni* might well have risen up against the godless invader. The
President of the Parthenopean Republic is said to have helped the
miracle along on that occasion by accompanying the archbishop to the
altar, where he showed him a pistol hidden under his coat and hissed
in his ear: 'Another minute, and you are a dead man!' The blood
liquefied without further ado; but the Neapolitans were so incensed at
their saint who had let himself be intimidated that they threw the vials
into the sea and transferred their devotion to Sant' Antonio instead.
When that saint failed to stop a subsequent eruption of Vesuvius, they
fished the vials out of the water and reinstated San Gennaro in his
customary honours. By then, the French had long beaten an orderly
retreat.)

There followed a period of violent repression during which Nelson, egged on by the twin furies of Maria Carolina and Emma Hamilton, tried to eradicate all vestiges of the Parthenopean Republic while the mob plundered the Jacobins' property—'*Chi tiene pan' e vino,*' they sang in the streets of Naples, '*Ha da esser Giaccobino*'—and the two husbands washed their hands of the whole business: Sir William was lamenting the loss of a part of his priceless collection of Pompeiiana which had gone down with *H.M.S. Colossus* while in transit to England, and Ferdinand had found the hunting near Palermo so to his liking that he could barely be persuaded to return to his subjects on the mainland. When the French gained the upper hand once more, after the Battle of Marengo, he was forced to grant an amnesty to the surviving republicans, to close all the ports of his kingdom to the British navy, and to allow a French army to be stationed deep in his territory, at Taranto. Even so, the Bourbons could consider themselves lucky. Napoleon, soon to be First Consul, had again treated them more leniently than his other and more powerful enemies. He was fully aware of Maria Carolina's abiding hatred of him, and there is respect as well as wit in his remark that she was 'the only man in the Kingdom of Naples'. It was only when he found out that she had been negotiating with Vienna with a view to joining the Third Coalition, that of 1805, that his patience gave out. After Austerlitz, he issued the famous proclamation 'The dynasty of Naples has ceased to reign' and placed his brother Joseph upon the throne, which Ferdinand had once again hastily vacated by retreating to his Sicilian hunting grounds.

Even though they had been repeatedly and ingloriously left in the lurch by their sovereign, the Neapolitans yet preserved a measure of affection for Ferdinand. The new king found his subjects unresponsive to French rule; Naples seethed with intrigue, and Joseph Bonaparte was not the man to suppress it. What was worse, he also lacked his brothers's military genius, so that the British were able to occupy Capri and display the Union Jack in full view of the mainland. Napoleon, Emperor of France by now and the undisputed master of Europe, thereupon ordered Joseph to assume the crown of Spain and to hand that of Naples over to Joachim Murat. From July 1808 until May 1815, this ex-cavalryman, a *beau sabreur* in plumes and spurs, ruled in

Naples at the side of his equally flamboyant wife, Caroline Bonaparte the Emperor's youngest sister, who made up in elegance what she may have lacked in chastity.

Having thus secured southern Italy, Napoleon turned his attention to the weightier problems of Spain and Russia, while his brother-in-law dislodged the British from Capri and bedazzled his subjects with parades and spectacles. The Bourbons, meanwhile, marked time in Sicily, where Ferdinand took a mistress and Maria Carolina (whose eldest daughter had become Empress of Austria) writhed in impotent fury when Napoleon, adding insult to injury, married Marie Louise in 1810 and made her, in her own words, 'the devil's grandmother'. After her death during a visit to Vienna in 1814, the widowed Ferdinand married in morganatic union his mistress, the Duchess of Floridia. In June of the following year, when Murat had fled after the collapse of the Empire, the Bourbon King re-entered Naples in triumph. The long nightmare was over, and the Congress of Vienna lost no time in confirming him sovereign of the reconstituted Kingdom of the Two Sicilies.

Strange as it may seem in view of the violence of these events, the restoration of Pompeii and Herculaneum had actually benefitted from the French occupation. Beginning with Championnet who had some buildings named after him in grateful recognition of his patronage,[9] the invaders turned out to be considerably more enterprising than the legitimate monarchs had been. Joseph Bonaparte made many visits to the excavations, revived the moribund Academy of Herculaneum, paid contractors a set fee for the removal from the site of a given amount of earth and ashes, and determined to put the whole undertaking on a sound financial basis by purchasing from its private owners the land under which some two-thirds of Pompeii still lay hidden. Lack of funds prevented the execution of this plan, which was to be partially realized by Murat; Joseph's other, equally well-intentioned projects also came to nought because he had entrusted them to A.C. Saliceti, the Minister of Police and most hated man in the land. Nevertheless, the digging had got underway again, and when Caroline Murat became Queen she stepped up its pace by bringing the work force up to a strength of several hundred (including detachments of the Neapolitan army, which preferred this duty to fighting in the snows of Russia), confirming the able Michele Arditi in his position as director of the museum while shrewdly leaving La Vega in nominal charge of the day-by-day operations, demanding weekly progress reports of them both, and subsidizing the publication of Mazois' *Les ruines de Pompéi* and of the engravings which Francesco Piranesi, Giovanni Battista's son, had made of the theatre of Herculaneum. All this activity bore impressive fruit. Many skeletons were found, although it was still not possible to preserve their molds for future generations; among the coins which were now for the first time brought to light in substantial numbers, there were numerous gold pieces from the reigns of Vespasian and Titus, freshly coined currency that had been dropped by its owners in their precipitate flight. The work was centred on the Street of Tombs, and it was here that a splendid monument was discovered on March 18, 1813, in the Queen's presence and that of the sculptor Canova: the tomb which a Greek lady by the mellifluous name of Naevolaeia Tyche had built for herself and her husband, the magistrate Munatius Faustus. It was found to contain glass amphorae with her ashes and those of her family, as well as humbler terra-cotta vessels in which those of her freedmen had been preserved.

Although its achievement fell far short of Chateaubriand's claims, the French interregnum was productive enough to rank with the great periods of Pompeiian archaeology, with the era of Winckelmann in the 1750s and 60s, that of Fiorelli in the 1860s, and that of Maiuri in the 1940s and 50s. There can be little doubt, furthermore, that the interest shown in the excavations by Madame de Staël on her only, and by Chateaubriand and Lamartine on their first trip to Pompeii was stimulated by the progress which was being made at that very time. Here again, one observes an unsuspected area of agreement between these writers and their *bête noire* Napoleon, who was known to be so partial to presents of archaeological origin that the Bourbons were able to play on this weakness by the well-timed offering of propitiatory gifts. As early as 1796, the revolutionary Directory had demanded and been granted the right to conduct excavations in Campania: however, when the Commissioner Faitpoult arrived in Naples in 1799 with the authority to confiscate, in the name of the French Republic, not only the lands and palaces belonging to the

Bourbons but even the treasures still resting under the soil of Pompeii and Herculaneum, Championnet (who was thereupon replaced by the less gentlemanly MacDonald) told him to leave the country within ten days. Lady Hamilton thus knew what she was doing when she preserved for Ferdinand, and shipped to Sicily along with the crown jewels, no fewer than fifty-two cases of exhibits from the Portici museum, which looked positively depleted when A. v. Kotzebue visited it in 1804. At another time, a 'package deal' was arranged between Paris and Palermo, by which the King gained some minor political concessions in exchange for a number of papyri from Herculaneum (and the services of his court musician Giovanni Paisiello, the first Consul's favourite composer, who now became a concert master in the Tuileries). These papyri, available in practically unlimited supply, easily transported, and potential bearers of scholarly prestige for any country whose experts could decipher them, paradoxically became objects of fervent interest to some of the dullest if highly placed minds of the time. In the years immediately preceding the French occupation, the Prince of Wales, the later George IV, had supported the investigations of J. Hayter, an English clergyman who unrolled and published a number of Philodemus' treatises as well as some fragments of Epicurus. In the 1820s, when Ferdinand wanted to stock the park of the Villa Floridiana with exotic fauna, the British envoy to Naples hit upon the idea of bartering a given number of papyri for as many—kangaroos.

After the Battle of Waterloo the British, who had been confined to their island for so many years, flooded the continent in successive waves of tourism which did not ebb until the latter half of the century. They introduced their hosts to foods and clothing and sports and customs which were soon absorbed, from beefsteak and plus fours to alpinism and five o'clock tea, by influential sections of the continental bourgeoisie. In many cases, they also brought with them their sense of civic freedom and dignity, a fine classical erudition, an advanced technological knowledge, and considerable wealth. In the Two Sicilies as elsewhere, the impact of this migration on an exhausted continent resulted in a period of English cultural hegemony. Those were the years in which Naples found her social historian in the Countess of Blessington, and Stendhal could write on the occasion of a royal ball that '*tout Londres était là*'; those were the years, also, in which Pompeii found its topographer and *cicerone* in Sir William Gell, a worthy successor to Winckelmann and Mazois, and its chief literary propagandist in Lord Lytton. At this stage of the proceedings, a word of caution is in order.

It is well to distinguish between the generic term of Romanticism and the leading Romantics as individuals. According to too many histories of literature, the movement began in England with the *Lyrical Ballads*, in Germany with the *Athenäum*, in France with *Hernani*, and is characterized by a 'subjective view of life and the self', the use of the *Doppelgängermotif*, a preference for nocturnal scenes and dream sequences, and the like. True as this may be, the whole truth is rather more complicated: it entails, among much else, the recognition that the great creators of this as of any other literary movement were both of their time and above it. The strange fate of Pompeii did, of course, stimulate much writing that is Romantic both in the picture-book and the textbook meaning of the term; we have already seen evidence of a tendency to find oneself in the object viewed, of a new awareness of national aspirations, of a pleasure in retrospection and mnemonic speculation, and we shall presently get our fill of 'worship of the past', 'fascination with death', 'yearning for the infinite', and other stock-in-trade items. Yet Pompeii is by no means a Romantic theme *par excellence;* for example, there is no glorification of the Middle Ages in the literature about this city whose very existence had been forgotten during those centuries, no backward glance to a time when the Christian and specifically the Roman faith was the prime mover of Man's actions (where Christianity does enter as a viable force, it represents not an old form of life in contrast to modern rationalism and liberalism, but a modern form of life in contrast to heathen cruelty and superstition), and little praising of the *Volk* by way of *costumbrismo, Heimatkunst,* or whatever. The Pompeiian literature of this period, and indeed all Romantic literature, may be likened to a mountain range whose peaks share with their lesser brethren a common base but not a common configuration.

One of the most formidable of these peaks is represented by George Gordon Lord Byron, but there is probably little reason to lament the fact that he never visited the Campanian excavations. Venice, Rome, Ravenna, Pisa, Bologna, and other cities found a place in *Childe Harold* and other works of the Italian years; Naples and Pompeii did not, partly because the poet thought that there was little to be gained by an excursion to southern Italy, a region which was likely to remain overshadowed in his mind by the previously undertaken visits to Greece and Constantinople. And he may well have been right. His familiarity with ancient history and art was too slight to have vouchsafed him such revelations as came to Goethe; to the conqueror of the Hellespont, the prospect of climbing Vesuvius cannot have presented a challenge; and those of his interests which were typical of the wellborn tourist of the time—folklore and local colour, a release from the social restraints prevailing at home, and a sense of participation in Italian affairs—had already been pre-empted by his literary, amatory, and political involvements in Venice, Ravenna, and Pisa. It was only after the death of his daughter Allegra and his friend Shelley that Byron seriously considered spending a winter in Naples (and adding a canto to *Childe Harold,* a task which was to be completed, after a fashion, by Lamartine). One can well imagine the stir which his arrival would have created, or the comments aroused by the retinue with which he travelled at the time: ten horses, three monkeys, five cats, eight dogs, an eagle, a crow, a falcon, and the incomparable Tita, his lordship's gondolier and bodyguard, in Shelley's estimate 'one of the most good-natured fellows I ever saw' even though he had stabbed two or three people. It would have been exciting, but it would also have been too late because Byron was too driven a man, by 1822, to have profited by an excursion to Naples and the excavations. At the time when he might have made that excursion, he was as close to death as Keats had been two years earlier when he had disembarked at Naples and been unable to go sightseeing, or as Sir Walter Scott would be a decade later, when he was escorted through Pompeii but was no longer capable of condensing his impressions on paper.

It remained for Percy Bysshe Shelley to do what Byron, Keats, and Scott had left undone. His development after settling in Italy in 1818 has aptly been compared to a butterfly breaking out of the chrysalis;[10] it might be added that no poet took so much from Italy and gave so much in return. He did not, like so many others, discover the country in the course of a Grand Tour: he found *himself* there during a sojourn of four years. His poetry, accordingly, transmutes rather than describes visual impressions, and one would be hard put to draw any conclusions about Florence from *Ode to the West Wind*, Rome from *Prometheus Unbound*, Como and the Baths of Lucca from *Rosalind and Helen*, Venice from *Julian and Maddalo*, Este from *Lines Written among the Euganean Hills*, or, for that matter, about Naples and Pompeii from the *Ode to Naples*. What these works do offer is some superb nature imagery, including possibly the finest sea-lyrics since Euripides, and an evocative power of which the Pompeiian reminiscence at the beginning of the *Ode to Naples* gives an example:

'I stood within the City disinterred;
　And heard the autumnal leaves like light footfalls
Of spirits passing through the streets; and heard
　The mountain's slumberous voice at intervals
Thrill through those roofless halls;
　The oracular thunder penetrating shook
The listening soul in my suspended blood;
　I felt that Earth out of her deep heart spoke—
I felt, but heard not: through white columns glowed
　The isle-sustaining ocean-flood,
A plane of light between two heavens of azure!'

The poem closes with the prophetic vision of an Italy which takes up arms against the 'crowned transgressors' from within and without. It is an indication of the variety of the creative impulses which Pompeii can activate in its visitors that this city, to which we owe the most chilling details about the ancient institution of slavery, should also have inspired a man like Shelley to this solemn, contrapuntally arranged paean to a movement which exhibited not a trace of ancient grandeur: the Neapolitan revolution of 1820, which collapsed shamefully as soon as the 'Anarchs of the North', i.e. the troops of the Holy Alliance, marched in, whereupon Ferdinand revoked the concessions which had been demanded of him and which he had granted with the remark: 'Yes, my children, I shall give you a Constitution, I shall even give you two . . .'[11]

The *Ode to Naples* is underscored, as it were, by the letter in which Shelley describes the visit recollected in the poem. Addressed to Thomas Love Peacock on January 26, 1819, it represents not only a worthy pendant to Walpole's report to Gray but an unstylized account of the impressions gathered by the poet, according to whose own statement the correspondence with Peacock was to take the place of an Italian diary. From the critical attitude toward contemporary life to the idealization of the Hellenic world and the attack on Christianity, it is as characteristic of its author as any 'Pompeiian' document. Furthermore, it adds to the theme a dimension which had hitherto been lacking—that of a natural setting considered not as a contrast to the city, as is the case in the many descriptions in which Pompeii appears as an object seen from without, but as a complement to it:

'. . . the glorious scenery around is not shut out, and . . . unlike the inhabitants of the Cimmerian ravines of modern cities, the ancient Pompeiians could contemplate the clouds and the lamps of heaven; could see the moon rise high behind Vesuvius, and the sun set in the sea, tremulous with an atmosphere of golden vapour, between Inarime [Ischia] and Misenum . . .'

The picture of Shelley in Pompeii is rounded out by a vignette from the pen of a young friend, Charles MacFarlane, who accompanied the poet through the excavations. Afterwards, they went to the shore and 'sat on a lava rock, with the sea almost washing our feet until sunset . . . My companion's expressive countenance was languid, despondent, melancholy, quite sad. He did not write them there— he certainly wrote nothing when I was with him, and was not the man to indulge in any such poetical affectations; but he *thought* here those thrilling verses which in the collection of his minor poems are called *Stanzas Written in Dejection, near Naples* . . . Yet—and because he was so impressionable, so thoroughly alive to external nature—we had scarcely got back to our very queer and very rapid conveyance than he rallied, joked in good Italian with our driver, and became most cheerful and facetious.'[12]

In view of the extraordinary magnetism which Italy has so long held for Germans, one would expect to find many references to the Campanian cities in the German literature of this time. And it is true that they are frequently mentioned by the poets of the Storm and Stress, Classicism, and Romanticism. Some, like Schiller in *Pompeji und Herkulanum* and Jean Paul in his novel *Titan*, wrote on them without ever having set eyes on the scene; others such as the Stolberg brothers and Carl Gustav Carus described them in terms of an entry in a travel journal; but only Goethe enriched the theme in a significant fashion and was in turn enriched by it.

Two explanations offer themselves for this astonishing barrenness in a literature which in other respects was more productive in the period 1770 to 1830 than before or since. From Heinse's *Ardinghello* (1787) to Mann's *Der Tod in Venedig* (1913) and *Doktor Faustus* (1947), Germans have tended to look at Italy from the artist's viewpoint, with the eyes of a painter, writer, musician (indeed, all German literature, not only that dealing with Italy, would be greatly impoverished if the genre of *Künstlerroman* were to be subtracted from the sum total of that literature). This was particularly the case in the period here under consideration; and if we add that the Romanticist preoccupation with the Middle Ages was stronger in Germany than elsewhere, we arrive at a partial solution of this riddle: Pompeii had little to offer to writers whose favourite fictional reincarnation was that of the medieval or Renaissance artist. To varying degrees, this applies to Novalis, Wackenroder, Tieck, Arnim, Brentano, and Eichendorff. Furthermore, the German Romantics travelled less than their French and English counterparts. They were thus unable, by and large, to expand with personal acquaintance such Pompeiian themes as their fertile imaginations may have suggested to them. The collective journeys of Madame de Staël, Chateaubriand, and Lamartine extended halfway around the world from Saint Petersburg to Niagara Falls and from Sweden to North Africa, while those of Eichendorff, Hölderlin, and E.T.A. Hoffmann extended from France to Poland; Byron, Shelley, and Keats lie buried far from their homeland, while Novalis, Wackenroder, and Brentano never left theirs. The Germans who did move about a little (among them Chamisso, Heine, and Platen) are far outweighed, in numbers and importance, by those of their compatriots who stayed put. In his long and active life Goethe undertook only one major journey, that to Italy in 1786–88, and never saw London, Paris, or even Vienna; Schiller, Beethoven, and Hegel did not leave the German language area, while Kant never stirred from his native city. Incalculable as the achievements of these men are, they were clearly not the result of a personal experience of the world at large. On the contrary: their lives give an impression of extraordinary sedentariness (a trait which came to be considered a virtue in the *Biedermeier*) and quite lack the element of worldly adventure which is so noticeable in the tradition of the writer-diplomat, one of the glories of French letters from the days of Chateaubriand and Lamartine to those of Paul Claudel and Saint-John Perse.

If Italian writers have barely been mentioned in these pages, it is because they paid little attention to Pompeii until Giacomo Leopardi making amends so to speak for a century of neglect, wrote *La Ginestra* (1836). Here, as in Shelley's *Ode to Naples,* a visit to the excavations sets in motion a train of philosophical reflections, although the Italian's conviction of the vanity of man's aspirations is as melancholy as the Englishman's dream of liberty had been cheerfully combative. Compared to the destructive forces of nature as these are exemplified by the volcano, human life is a paltry thing—especially when it is given a false sense of permanence through that belief in mankind's measured ascent toward perfection, in *le magnifiche sorti e progressive,* which was as dear to nineteenth-century Liberalism as it was odious to Leopardi. This life of ours is likened to that of an ant-heap which is as quickly destroyed by a falling apple as Pompeii was wiped out by Vesuvius, the mountain which perpetually threatens an existence which is none-theless perpetually regenerated in its shade—a thought reminiscent of the Prologue to Goethe's *Faust* and of Pascal's remark that 'Even if it were to annihilate him, the universe would still not be as noble as man'.[13] Even now, eighteen hundred years after the city's destruction, the peasant trimming his vines will anxiously lift up his glance to the volcano, ready for instantaneous flight if the lava should flow again and light up nocturnal Naples and the distant shore of Capri (the picture is taken from reality because the old man who had witnessed the eruption of 1817 and told Leopardi about it, was still so terror-struck that he would not turn his back to the mountain). The most becoming manner in which we can face life is that symbolized by the *ginestra*, the humble broom growing on the lava fields where it will one day be blotted out by a new cataclysm. Unlike man, the flower does not pretend to have been granted immortality; unlike man, it lives for the day, humbly and wisely like a Rilkean 'thing'.

Part meditation, part idyll, part satire, the poem expresses an apocalyptic view of life interspersed with cascading images of the kind that a drowning man is said to have of his own individual existence. Presentiments of death as well as the circumstances in which he found himself at the time—in a friend's house near Torre d'Annunziata, where he had sought refuge from the cholera in Naples—presumably heightened Leopardi's susceptibility to this theme, which is here developed in several aspects: the historical one of human progress, the metaphysical one of a life lived in the shadow of death (which is present already in De Brosses and now become a distinct part of the Pompeiian motif), the ethical one of composure in the face of tragedy, and the poetic one of the fragrant little flower, the description of which brackets the poem and gives it a formal unity.

After the Spanish dramatist Leandro Fernández de Moratín had set down his impressions of Pompeii in the late eighteenth century, his compatriot Francisco Martínez de la Rosa, in attempting to console a friend for the loss of his wife in the *Epistola al duque de Frías en la muerte de su esposal* now draws comfort from his own reflections made during a visit to Pompeii. Written in 1830, the elegy anticipates Leopardi's poem in the writer's existential isolation brought about by a recent journey to the excavations, in the conclusion drawn from this experience:

> '*Qué pequeño, que mísero y mezquino*
> *el mundo ante mis ojos parecía*
> *cuando me hallaba allí . . .!*'

and above all in the realization that the world resignedly accepts its loss, whether it be that of an entire city or the death of a beloved person. What is lacking in his elegy is the element of satire so pronounced in

Leopardi's work; it would have agreed neither with the Spaniard's belief in political action not with the religious basis of his poem.

Leopardi dealt with Pompeii not only in *La Ginestra,* the 'richest, most comprehensive, and in regard to the author's personality the most significant of his works',[14] but in the third canto of the *Paralipomeni della Batracomiomachia*. In this parody both of the classical epic and of politics (the mice represent the Neapolitans who had risen up in 1820, the frogs the equally despised subjects of the Papal States, the crabs the Austrians), he describes Topaia, the mouse state's subterranean capital in which one can find one's way only with the aid of torches, as in Herculaneum, which to the shame of all Italy still lies hidden under 'the tawdry inns and houses' of Resina. Pompeii, too— he adds bitingly—would have been excavated long ago had it rested in German or British soil. In his attack on the staff of the Portici Museum, that 'hypocritical gang'—*ipocrita canaglia*—which kept the world waiting so long for a deciphering of the papyri, Leopardi is so swept away by hatred that he has to bring himself back forcibly to the subject at hand: 'But let us return to the mice . . .'

By thus referring to the city in an animal epic, Leopardi introduces Pompeii into a genre of venerable age, a phenomenon which may also be observed elsewhere in late Romanticism. At the time when Pompeii was *raised* to the rank of a theme prominently treated by great writers in important works, it was also *broadened* into one which was to be joined, by Gautier, Bulwer, and Jensen, to some of the oldest traditions in all literature. Within a century, it thus grew from an occasional entry in a travel log to a narrative episode and eventually to the basic theme of a number of significant poems. It now becomes the focus of entire novels and therewith enters into the mainstream of world literature.

3 Antique bas-relief from the Chiaramonti collection.
Fragment of no. 1284. Musei Vaticani, Rome.

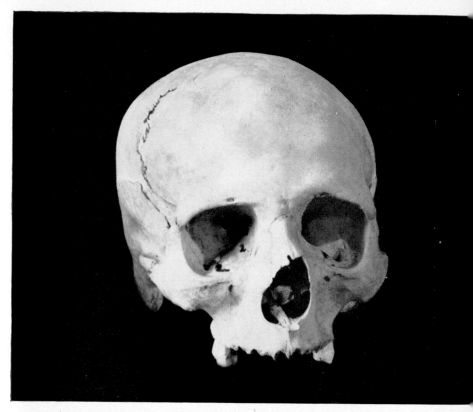

14a *Above* The skull of Arbaces from Bulwer-Lytton's home at Knebworth, Hertfordshire.

14b *Below* Corpse of a Pompeiian, killed while trying to flee.

4

Arbaces' Skull, Arria's Bosom, Gradiva's Foot

'Neither of us are in love with Italy, and therefore I devoutly
hope that we may be back in dear England by the end of
December. The travelling here may be divided into three
classes: plague, pestilence, and famine. Plague—the mos-
quitoes, Pestilence—the smells, and Famine—the dinners . . .
Poets ought to be strangled for all the lies they have told of
this country.'

Mrs Edward Bulwer to Miss Greene,
Florence, October 14, 1833

LEAVING ASIDE for now the various subsidiary plots, the story of
Edward Bulwer's *The Last Days of Pompeii* is quickly recounted.

The handsome young Athenian Glaucus, long a resident of Pompeii,
loves Ione, who lives with her brother Apaecides in her own house but
under the supervision of a guardian. The latter, the Egyptian Arbaces,
wishes to marry the girl and attempts to discredit his younger rival in
her eyes. When this miscarries, he joins forces with the daughter of the
nouveau riche Diomedes, the beautiful Julia, who would like to see
Glaucus among her own throng of admirers. From an Etrurian
sorceress who plies her trade in a cave on Mount Vesuvius, Arbaces
procures a love potion which he hands over to Julia with a recommendation that she use it on Glaucus (whereupon Ione, bereft of her
lover, would fall prey to Arbaces himself). In reality, the potion is a
colourless and odourless poison designed to render its victim temporarily insane.

The Athenian, however, is loved not only by Ione and Julia but
(unbeknownst to him) also by the blind slave girl Nydia, who steals the
vial from Julia's house and empties its contents into the water drunk
by the unsuspecting young man. As a result, Glaucus does indeed lose
his reason. Wandering about like a madman in the nocturnal streets of
Pompeii, he is unfortunate enough to happen upon the scene as

Arbaces waylays and kills his ward Apaecides because the latter had betrayed the mysteries of Isis and become a Christian. It is an easy matter for the Egyptian to press the murder weapon into the babbling Glaucus' hand, and to convince the people who come running up that Glaucus had committed the murder and that he, Arbaces, had caught him at it. The Athenian is arrested and convicted the more quickly as gladiatorial games have been scheduled, and the Pompeiians had been wishing for some time to have a condemned criminal in their jail whom they might pit against a lion. The reluctant gladiator is now found: the innocent Glaucus, who has meanwhile recovered his reason and vainly denies having killed Apaecides, is sentenced to fight in the arena against the beast, which has already been put on starvation rations. With the exception of the epicurean Sallust, all the gay young blades who had been his friends now turn their backs on Glaucus. Arbaces has meanwhile lured Ione and Nydia to his house, where they are held prisoner together with Calenus, a priest of the goddess Isis who had witnessed the deed and rashly threatened to expose the real culprit. At the last moment, when the Egyptian has already left for the amphi-theatre with his slaves and retinue in order to watch Glaucus' ordeal, Nydia manages to send a message to Sallust, who thereupon frees the prisoners. Glaucus and the lion are already facing each other in the arena when Calenus suddenly enters and explains to the startled *praetor* what had really happened: Arbaces had killed Apaecides and put the blame on Glaucus, in order to rid himself of both men and to force the reluctant Ione to become his wife after all.

The games are interrupted, and the bloodthirsty public is about to seize the wily Egyptian in order to have *him* fight the lion, when Vesuvius erupts and sends its ashes over the city. Arbaces, Calenus, Julia, and countless others find their death in the general catastrophe while Nydia, who, being blind, knows every nook and corner of Pompeii by heart and is not confused by the sudden darkness, leads Glaucus and Ione to the shore. They make their escape on board a departing vessel, but early the next morning, when they are safely on the high seas, Nydia quietly slips overboard and disappears beneath the waves. She has saved her lover and is now selfless enough to leave him, the well-born Athenian to whose affection she (who gave him the potion) has no right, to the lovely Ione. Ten years later, Glaucus sends Sallust the letter with which the story ends. He invites his friend to visit him and Ione in Athens, where they live happily united and in grateful remembrance of the blind slave girl to whom they owe their life and happiness.

Despite its sticky sentimentality ('How beautiful,' said Glaucus in a half-whispered tone, 'is that expression by which we call Earth our Mother!'), its stilted language ('Daughter of Etruria, whither wendest thou?'), and its many violations of historical truth, this story, one of the most famous of all novels, possesses some interest and dramatic tension even for the modern reader. One of the reasons for its survival lies in the author's skill in combining the roles of involved spectator and omniscient narrator. Instead of launching into a detailed description of Pompeii, he has the novel open with a dialogue of such liveliness and immediacy that it might have been spoken, *mutatis mutandis*, in the London of the eighteen-twenties. Bulwer philosophizes on occasion, although his skiff sails but lightly burdened across the seas of reflection ('It is in these, the lesser intrigues of life, that we mostly find ourselves at home with the past'); sometimes he turns political ('Italy, Italy . . . listen not to the blind policy which would unite all your crested cities'), and at other times expresses what one suspects are highly idiosyncratic views, as in the curse hurled by the sorceress at Glaucus and Ione when they stand before her, at the witching hour and in the full bloom of love: 'It is a pleasure to the old and withered to look upon young hearts like yours . . . and to know that the time will come when you will loathe each other . . . loathe . . . loathe . . . ha! ha! ha!' (It was in that winter of 1833-34 that the marriage of Edward and Rosina Bulwer broke up and they, too, began to loathe one another.) Now and then he stands back altogether from his story and regards from a distance the tapestry he has just woven: 'Meanwhile Fulvius,' one such passage reads, 'the Roman poet whom his contemporaries declared immortal, and who, but for this history, would never have been heard of in our neglectful age, came . . .' Ironic interludes of this nature anticipate Thomas Mann's 'Did we already mention that . . . ?' and add a welcome pinch of salt to a diet which would otherwise be all too bland. Nor are the often arbitrary comparisons between Pompeii and modern Paris or Westminster, or the occasional displays of learned pedantry ('Archimagiris,' we are told in a footnote, 'was the lofty title of the chief cook [in Pompeiian mansions]'), as bothersome as they might be in a less skillfully constructed novel. They are so artfully built into this narrative that they do not appreciably retard its flow.

Bulwer's treatment of the historical and archaeological background may be summed up by saying that the environment in which the story unfolds is realistically drawn while the story itself is pure invention. Even the figure of Diomedes, based on the Arrius Diomedes whose villa was to serve as the locale of a number of prose works set in Pompeii, is in essence an invented figure because so little is known about the historical bearer of that name (in contrast to such Pompeiians as Naevolaeia Tyche or the priestess Eumachia) that it is now thought that the villa had not belonged to him at all but to a patrician. We have already seen that the populace was *not* assembled in the amphitheatre when the disaster struck, and that such Christian congregations as may have existed in Pompeii cannot have been as numerous and influential as depicted by this author. Nevertheless, *se non è vero è ben trovato:* poetic imagination proved more fruitful than historical fact, and the most obviously 'invented' figures, Arbaces and the fearless Christian Olinthus, were to find more literary successors than the less unbeliev-able lovers or even poor Nydia. Both the figure of the heathen fiend and the contrasting one of the true believer who reproaches his carefree fellow-citizens with their sins (and is later saved from the common ruin by divine intervention) are archetypes of mythical and biblical origin which could not fail to be transplanted, sooner or later, to Campania. That the time was ripe just then is indicated by the publication, also in 1834, of *Herculanum, ou l'orge romaine* by Joseph Méry of Mar-seilles. In that poem, an old Jewish slave interrupts a revel expressly organized to mark the destruction of Jerusalem, by announcing that Herculaneum's last hour had also struck:

> *'Dieux grands! Dieux immortels! C'est notre heure dernière!*
> *Les pins sont secoués ainsi qu'une crinière;*
> *Le Vésuve indigne rugit comme un lion;*
> *N'offense pas les Dieux, écoute, ô Pollion!'*

Unrepentant, Pollion and his companions continue their carousal until

they are swallowed up by the earth, upon which there remains only
the Jew:

'*Sur Herculanum mort vit un hébreu vivant !*'

(Méry, not by chance a good friend of Dumas *père*, later enlarged these
cinematographic effects in an opera on Herculaneum, performed in
1859 with music by Félicien David.)

Bulwer's fictitious heroes, then, act in a setting which is drawn as
precisely as the state of the excavations and his own topographical
knowledge permitted. The amphitheatre is not that of Verona or
Syracuse, but unmistakeably that of Pompeii. The house of the fictitious Glaucus corresponds in every detail to the real one of the Tragic
Poet, whose garden and *lararium* are described as lovingly as the fresco
of 'Achilles and Briseis' which had already impressed Goethe and now
elicits from Bulwer the kind of rhetorical question usually asked not by
a novelist but by a tourist guide: 'Who does not acknowledge the force,
the vigour, the beauty employed in delineating the forms and faces of
Achilles and the immortal slave?' The Villa of Diomedes and the
Temple of Isis are described in the same Baedeker style; indeed the
author's enthusiasm extends even to objects like the slate-pencil which
serves as murder weapon (here, Bulwer remarks that Julius Caesar, too,
was stabbed with just such a stylus carried in the belt) and the portable
kitchen stoves used in some ancient households: 'An admirable
contrivance of this nature,' he writes with disarming naïveté, 'may still
be seen in the Neapolitan Museum.' His love of detail respects only
two limits: the indecent pictures, and of course all that part of Pompeii
which still lay hidden under the earth. He would not otherwise have
missed commenting on the frescoes in the Villa of the Mysteries, which
were not discovered until 1930.

Such writing strikes the modern reader, whose palate is accustomed
to fare of very different texture, as artificial and stale: as Victorian,
which indeed it is. Yet the reader has no cause for complaint since he
is warned at the very beginning that it is the author's intention 'to
people once more those deserted streets'.[1] One would however be
inclined to assume, from such an arbitrary compounding of fact and
fiction, that Bulwer had carried away from Pompeii impressions quite
different from those found in other authors. Yet this is by no means

the case. He adds to the theme some personal touches, such as the stress laid on astrology, and some motifs of a generically Romantic nature as in the figure of the sorceress, which contrasts oddly enough with the emanations of a Platonic spirit that Madame de Staël claimed to have sensed in Pompeii thirty years before; but in general, he merely repeats what others had said earlier. Like Walpole and Gray, he quotes the ancients, Horace's *Persicos odi* and much else; the observation that 'the Baths at Pompeii differed, of course, in plan and construction from the vast and complicated thermae of Rome' could as well stem from Chateaubriand or some other writer struck by this discrepancy; the confrontations of ancient with modern customs, for example in relation to manners ('. . . our refined English notions, which place good breeding in indifference . . .') remind one of Shelley, and the references to Pliny and Dio Cassius are not original either. Bulwer's contribution to Pompeiian literature thus lies neither in his description of the city nor in the story as such, a rather common love story with jealousy, crime, and happy end, nor yet in the juxtaposition of various personality types which reveal their true nature only in the face of death; this had already been done by Delphine Gay, the later Madame de Girardin, in her poem *Le dernier jour de Pompéi* (1828). What is signally new is the animation of this setting, or in Bulwer's own phrase the 'peopling' of the city's deserted streets, with two different sets of characters: some of an original cast and others of a traditional derivation, both of which serve to introduce Pompeii into narrative literature at large. Foremost among the originals is Nydia, the blind slave girl, a brilliantly conceived figure for which the author was 'indebted to a casual conversation with a gentleman well known amongst the English at Naples for his general knowledge of the many paths of life.'[2] Glaucus, too, is an individual, despite many a trait reminiscent of other literary heroes and possible models: despite a charming nonchalance which brings to mind Goethe's Egmont, a melancholy akin to that of Madame de Staël's Oswald, and a not ignoble idleness—less a character trait than a burden imposed by the times—which reminds one of certain heroes of Stendhal. Another man who is *ben trovato* is young Lydon, the gladiator who fights in the arena only in order to purchase his father's freedom, and is promptly slain by an adversary whose self-reliance is not weakened by reflections upon the meaning of it all. Among the figures which are not individualized but derived from a literary tradition, that of Arbaces is most forcefully drawn: an outsider in Pompeii much like Glaucus, he is not seen positively like the young Athenian who conquers all hearts (and is as blond as one expects such a protagonist to be), but demonized as a swarthy Egyptian driven by monstrous ambitions and yet controlled by cold reflection. Despite his Levantine rather than Latin origin he clearly belongs to that tradition of the devilish Southerner which was so popular in the Romantic period, into the rogues' gallery represented by the group Borgia-Cellini-Cenci-Casanova, figures which were so ubiquitous at the time that Paul de Musset expected to find in Italy 'des brigands partout, a jealous husband behind every wall, with a dagger in his hand; in every sleeve a stiletto, poison in every bottle, a cicisbeo or cavalier servente by every lady's side. This stylized Italy, the Frenchman discovered with a sigh of relief, 'exists only in Ann Radcliffe's novels, and she invented it on the foggy shores of the Thames'.[3] It is through Arbaces, above all, that Pompeii now takes its place in Satanic literature, which will be discussed later.

Given the great popularity of this novel, it is not surprising that the figure of Arbaces eventually transcended the very bounds of literature, and that the ceremonies of the Isis cult which the Egyptian is shown performing should, for example, have so impressed Madame Blavatsky, the founder of the Theosophic Society, that she detailed them in Isis Unveiled and adopted them for the movement's ritual.[4] Bulwer's Diomedes and his wanton daughter, on the other hand, are no more than empty shades which later writers were to borrow and fill out as it suited their purposes. Both occur again in Gautier's novel Arria Marcella (1852) and in Ferdinand Gregorovius' Euphorion—eine Dichtung aus Pompeji (1858), a painfully stilted epic in neoclassical form:

'Lied, eh' weiter du eilest mit der wechselnden Lampe des Lebens,
Tritt zu den fernen Geliebten mir froh, und der sanften Olive
Kränze verteile und sprich: Heil, Edele, Wenige, Heil euch!
Die in der Brust ihr noch idealische Flammen ernähret,
Abhold Eitelm und Feinde der dunkelen Tagesgewohnheit . . .'

in which the father becomes the very model of an enterprising business-man, while his daughter resembles the demure Ione, whose name she bears, rather than Bulwer's imperious Julia.

Bulwer had been inspired to write his novel not only by his talks with Sir William Gell and the archaeologist Antonio Bonucci but by a painting, 'The Last Day of Pompeii', which he had seen when passing through Milan. What actually made him set pen to paper had been the inspection of skeletons found on the site, and it is indeed remarkable how precisely the situation in which these had been discovered was later mirrored in the end met by Calenus, Diomedes, Arbaces, and others in the novel (which Bulwer evidently composed in the manner in which crime stories are written, so that one is able to deduce, from the state and position of the body, the victim's last movements in life). The author had been especially impressed by a skull from the shape and measurements of which he assumed that it must have housed the brain of an extraordinarily gifted man. This grisly relic, the 'Skull of Arbaces', later adorned the desk in his study at Knebworth.

Among the eighteen corpses found 1771-4 in the Villa of Diomedes had been that of a young woman, of whose hip and bosom a cast was taken at the time. Since we take leave of Julia in the cellar of that house, where she had sought refuge from the ashes with her family and slaves, Bulwer probably drew on this particular find when he described her end. In *Arria Marcella*, Théophile Gautier adds another chapter to the fictional history of this woman, of whom nothing is known beyond the fact that she possessed a '*magnifique sein de femme*' (Dumas *père*)— an endowment to which she owes an immortality not vouchsafed to the inventor of the wheel, or to countless other benefactors of mankind who will remain forever nameless.

In Gautier's story, three young Frenchmen visit the Museo degli Studii (now Nazionale) in Naples. While Max and Fabio are busy looking at other exhibits, Octavian stops before a glass case containing a heap of coagulated ashes on which is imprinted the outline of a young woman's breasts and hip. It had been found in Pompeii where it had cooled, almost two thousand years before, around the victim's form. Awakening Octavian from his reverie, Max and Fabio leave the museum with him and take the train to Pompeii. There they are taken in tow by a guide—in F.C. de Sumichrast's translation, 'a guide took them, a mishap which it is hard to avoid in Italy . . . *un guide les prit, calamité qu'il est difficile de conjurer en Italie*'. Although they had heard much about Pompeii, they are overwhelmed by the experience of actually being there. The sensitive Octavian, in particular, is touched by the evidence of a vanished life which he sees all about him: the ruts worn in the pavement, the graffiti of playbills and advertisements, the temples and taverns and theatres. They walk along the Street of Tombs (not without being reminded, as well-read young men, of Goethe's somewhat trite observation that 'the pagans adorned the sarcophagi with the images of life') and continue their tour with a thorough visit of the Villa of Diomedes. In the cellar of that building, Octavian is moved by the guide's remark that they were standing in the very spot where the remains of the woman had been found whose cast is preserved in the museum: 'The death of a mistress or of a friend could not have affected him more deeply, and when Max and Fabio had turned away, a tear fell, two thousand years late, on the spot where that woman, for whom he yearned with a retrospective love, had been stifled by the volcano's hot cinders.' The others, however, have had their fill of sightseeing. '*Assez d'archéologie comme cela!*' exclaims Fabio as he dismisses the guide, 'we do not intend to write a dissertation on a pitcher or a tile dating back to Caesar's time, in order to have ourselves elected to some provincial academy.' Cutting short the tour, the three friends repair to an inn for dinner and a night's rest.

Before going to their rooms, they sit about at the table drinking and talking of women. Fabio insists that they be pretty; money, education, and social standing are matters of no concern to him. Max, on his part, relishes the *difficulté vaincue* of successful flirtation and tends to lose interest once he has made his conquest. The romantic Octavian, however, is concerned not with the living, but with the evocation of past passions. He has assembled in his mind '*un sérail idéal avec Sémiramis, Aspasie, Cléopâtre, Diane de Poitiers, Jeanne d'Aragon*'; in fact his necrophilic propensities are so strong that he had once attempted to recall to life, with a spiritualist's aid, a dead lady of whom he possessed a lock of hair.

Their heads heavy with Falernian, Max and Fabio retire for the night. But Octavian finds no sleep. He leaves the inn, and, raising the wooden bar which then marked the city's boundaries, goes for a walk in nocturnal Pompeii. He soon fancies that he hears voices and perceives human shapes stealthily moving about in the ruins. When the sun rises, it shines on a city which is intact: not restored, but undestroyed. Octavian, a Frenchman of the nineteenth century, finds himself in the midst of the bustling city which presently unfolds itself before his eyes as it might have looked on a market day in the reign of the Emperor Titus. When he discovers that his dream of being transported back into bygone ages has become reality, if perhaps only for a few hours, it occurs to him that the woman whose form he had admired in the museum must also be among the living, and possibly not far away. Walking along the street, he falls in with a young man who is as much taken aback by his garb—'the ghastly modern hat, an ugly black frock-coat, his legs encased in trousers'—as we would be if we encountered a Red Indian sauntering on the boulevards of Paris. Although conversation is difficult because Octavian speaks Latin with a Gaul's intonation, the Pompeiian invites his friend from the provinces to accompany him to the theatre, where Plautus' *Casina* is to be given that afternoon.

During the performance Octavian chances to see, in the women's section, a dark-haired young woman with soft eyes and a passionate mouth. Her arms are bare, 'and from the tips of her proud breasts which raised the mauve-coloured tunic, fell two folds which might have been carved in marble by Phidias or Cleomenes. The sight of these breasts, so perfect in shape and faultless in outline, filled Octavian with emotion. It seemed to him that they exactly fitted the hollow mould in the Naples museum. His heart told him that this was the woman who had suffocated in the ashes of Vesuvius, in the Villa of Arrius Diomedes.'

Returning Octavian's admiring glances with equal ardour, the young woman whispers something to the slave girl seated beside her. The play is no sooner over than the latter introduces herself as the servant of Arria Marcella and peremptorily tells Octavian: '*Ma maîtresse vous aime, suivez-moi.*' Led by the girl, the young Frenchman now traverses sections of Pompeii which he had not seen when visiting the city as a tourist the previous day because they had not yet been excavated (!). However, he is no longer interested in archaeology; he has eyes only for a bosom which has triumphed over the ages. In the villa he is handed over to slaves who bathe, rub, and perfume him, and clothe him in a white tunic. When the maid returns, she leads him to the chamber where Arria awaits him, reclining in tempting disarray on a *biclinium* with her '*poitrine laissée à demi découverte par le pli negligé d'un peplum*'. Taking up the seat by her side, Octavian eats the delicacies offered by Asiatic slaves, while Arria amorously whispers that his love for her has proved to be so strong that it has bridged the centuries and brought her back to life. When the slaves have removed the table, Octavian vows eternal love to the beautiful Arria. Suddenly an old man bursts into the room; he wears a brown coat and has a small cross hanging from his neck. His face is severe and his manner commanding. The unwelcome guest is her father, Arrius Diomedes, who—in complete contrast to that figure in Bulwer's novel—has taken up the new faith in the midst of the heathen city. 'Have two thousand years not calmed you?' he scolds his daughter, 'Do your wanton arms still draw to your soulless marble bosom the poor madmen bewitched by your magic?' Still in her lover's embrace, Arria pleads in vain: '*Ne me replongez pas dans la pâle néant!*' With a mighty curse pronounced to a distant bell ringing the Ave Maria, the old man exorcises and changes her, before the horrified Octavian's eyes, back into the heap of bones and ashes that had been found when the building was excavated. The Frenchman, unconscious, is later found by Max and Fabio who had become alarmed at his disappearance; he tells them only that he must have fainted while walking through the city at night. They return to Naples and eventually to Paris, where Octavian later marries a lovely young Englishwoman. It is ostensibly a happy match, but his bride feels, '*avec cet instinct du coeur que rien ne trompe*', that Octavian nurtures in his heart a love deeper than that which he has for her. She suspects that he keeps a mistress, but can find no evidence of one . . . 'but then, she would never have dreamt of being jealous of Arria Marcella, daughter of Arrius Diomedes, a freedman of Tiberius'.

Arria Marcella is a well-told story worthy of its author, the '*poète impeccable* [*et*] *parfait magicien ès lettres*' to whom Baudelaire dedicated *Les fleurs du mal*. It contains dream sequences and hallucinatory passages reminiscent of Poe, and evocations of a past civilization which are briefer but no less effective than those found in Hugo's *Notre Dame de Paris* or Flaubert's *Salammbô*. These traits, along with the vampire motif and a strong indebtedness to Goethe's *Faust* (which Gautier's friend Gérard de Nerval had just translated) serve to anchor the work firmly in the mid-nineteenth century. But it is more than just another Romantic ghost story; it also bears the mark of the author's particular genius. For if E.T.A. Hoffmann was at heart a musician, Gautier, who had studied painting before taking up the pen, remained a *peintre manqué* who describes the city as it appeared on a brilliant summer morning, when 'owing to the sun's splendour and the transparency of the air, objects take on a colouring which would be considered fabulous in the North'. The occasional flashes of a Byronic wit—when the three friends laugh out aloud over something in the museum, they arouse 'the great disgust of the taciturn English and of the stolid tourists busily turning over their guidebooks'—are likewise in keeping with the spirit of this knight of the *gilet rouge* who had so distinguished himself at the première of *Hernani*. Although not a learned man, the poet possessed a somewhat journalistic but genuine love of recondite scholarly detail. This predilection shines through on almost every page, whether he quotes Boileau, paraphrases Hamlet's 'Imperious Caesar, dead and turn'd to clay', nonchalantly speaks of the *impluvium, exedra,* and *nymphaeum* of the Villa of Diomedes, or attempts to render more plausible Octavian's evocation of his mistress by reference to Faust's yearning for Tyndarus' daughter and to the silken sails of Cleopatra's barge, which still swell, in the minds of some passionate and nostalgic men, 'on some blue ideal Cydnus'.

Aside from making pleasant reading for its own sake, *Arria Marcella* is interesting on account of its historical position: it stands astride the point of intersection, so to speak, of several cultural co-ordinates. The theme of a man's infatuation with a female statue which arises out of the totemistic practices of primitive societies (and is related to the prohibition, in Judaism and Mohammedanism, of pictorial representations of the godhead), has fascinated writers of many lands and ages. In ancient literature, it was treated by Lucian and above all by Ovid, where Pygmalion's desire is happily fulfilled when the goddess of love, having breathed life into the ivory statue which he has fashioned, presides over the marriage feast. In the Middle Ages the statue no longer symbolizes the dream projection of an innocent girl. It now comes to represent Woman as a satanic creature and the source of all evil, often in the guise of Venus, whose wantonly sexual aspect as *Venus Meretrix* had been stressed, by a majority of the Church Fathers, to the exclusion of the more positive attributes which had belonged to her in earlier times (a divergence of values mirrored in the contrast between 'veneration' and 'venereal', from Sanskrit *van*=to wish, to desire). The man now loses his soul or even his life over this infatuation for a statue, which, inhabited by the devil himself or at any rate thoroughly demonized, comes to life at a given stage in the courtship. This moment is frequently marked by the performing of a ritual act of betrothal such as the placing of a ring on her extended finger, a formality which may seal the lover's fate as irreversibly as that of the medieval Faust was sealed when he signed his name, in blood, under the compact with the devil (who, in turn, helped him perform a similar act of statue-magic in bringing back to life Helen of Troy, an embodiment of feminine allure second only to Venus herself). In some versions, the man places the ring on the statue's finger by chance or in jest, as in Thomas Moore's *The Ring*, where Rupert, about

> 'To strike the bounding tennis ball
> In feat and manly sport,'

looks for a place where he might leave

> 'The wedding ring so bright,
> Which was to grace the lily hand
> Of Isabel that night.
> And fearing he might break the gem,
> Or lose it in the play,
> He looked around the court, to see
> Where he the ring might lay.'

He decides that an ancient statue—found, in those pre-Wimbledon days, on the court itself— would make a good place for safekeeping, and proceeds with the game. But the unwary suitor is caught when the statue crooks her finger:

'But, oh! how he was shocked to find
The marble finger bent!'

Rupert (and many a less athletic hero in the same predicament) can no longer retrieve the ring because this would be tantamount to breaking a troth which has been plighted, even if unwittingly. Unless she is exorcised by a magician, or a saint as in Moore's poem, the statue woman will ruin her lover or at the very least prevent, by her jealous and tactless presence on the wedding night, the consummation of any legal and Christian marriage which the man may meanwhile have contracted.

In a number of variations decreed by the personality, intention, and period of the respective author, this motif of the statue wedding (with or without ring, for the pronouncing of a spell will produce the same effect) occurs in many lands. In more recent English literature, it is found not only in Moore, but in William Morris and Walter Pater; in France, it occurs in Gautier (*La morte amoureuse* as well as *Arria Marcella*), Mérimée, Flaubert, and D'Annunzio in his French phase; in German literature it plays a role in Goethe, Brentano, Hoffmann, Eichendorff, Heine, Hauptmann, and others; in the United States, it may be found in Hawthorne's *Marble Faun* and Wilder's *Cabala*. Its temporal dimension is bracketed by William of Malmesbury's *De gestis regum Anglorum* (ab. 1125) and Günter Grass' *Die Blechtrommel* (1958), while its moral dimension extends from the stern warning against the temptations of the flesh embodied in the medieval German *Kaiserchronik* to the bizarre anecdote told about the statue of Justitia atop the tomb of Pope Paul III in St Peter's: 'If the absurd rumour that a Spaniard had misbehaved [with this statue] should be true, then this must have been an exceedingly coarse-minded fellow. Yet this Justice was in truth seated quite nakedly, as fat as a Dutch whore and in a most provocative position, in the most sacred spot of St Peter's, until a pontiff with a sense of decorum [Urban VIII] caused a brass veil to be thrown over her lap [the designer of this unusual *cache-sexe* was Bernini], so that only her thighs were left exposed to the contemplation of future Spaniards.'[5]

'Decent' and 'indecent' having become somewhat relative terms, we shall not delve deeply into the role which Pompeii has played in the history of pornographic literature. Suffice it to say that *pompeiiana* have long occupied a place of honour in collections of erotica. The city is so often considered as representative of Roman culture as a whole that these objects have come to possess, along with their libidinous attractions, some legitimate scientific value. In a well-known epistle to Bianconi, Winckelmann had already described a priapic statuette whose right hand makes an expressive gesture while the raised left *'fa la fica'* (to which the archaeologist characteristically added 'with which you are more familiar than I am'); the Comte de Caylus was equally outspoken, but that had been, after all, in rococo days. At the dawn of the Victorian age, however, Bulwer also felt constrained to mention some priapic objects, at least in passing, while Gautier speaks both of the coloured terra cotta phallus with the legend *'Hic habitat felicitas'* and the Pompeiian shop where small golden priapi were sold, 'such as are still to be found in Naples, as defence against *jettatura'*. Details of this nature are not necessarily salacious. They belong to the Pompeiian theme, and as one leafs through Roux Aîné's and M.L. Barré's *'Recueil général des peintures, bronzes, mosaïques etc. découverts . . . à Herculanum et à Pompéei'*, one cannot help observing that such notions of the sexual life of the ancients as have come down to us through literature are fragmentary in the extreme, and that the interest taken in these details even by otherwise prudish visitors is in many cases entirely legitimate. This aspect of Pompeii is not limited to documenting such well-known facets of ancient culture as paederasty or hermaphroditism; it encompasses much else, for example an explanation of the frequency—which according to the evidence presented by Pompeiian drawings, must have been high—of a third party's presence during coitus, on the mythological level (Apollo accompanying on the lyre the loveplay of Bacchus and Ariadne) as well as in real life (a female slave handing to a copulating couple a goblet containing refreshment, on the nature of which there has been much speculation). The above collection of paintings and bronzes, based on the *Antichità d'Ercolano* and supplemented by material kept under lock and key in the Secret Museum at Naples, was published in the 1840s and predictably set a number of 'racey' hack writers to extolling the libidinous aspects of life in ancient Pompeii.

Related to this theme and that of the statue-wedding is yet another motif touched upon in *Arria Marcella:* that of Italy as the home of beauty and the abode of evil. The long line of artists who have felt drawn to the country on account of its art, landscape, music, climate, etc., is too famous to require enumeration here; Gautier has taken his place in that line both with his novel and with *Voyage en Italie*. Less celebrated but equally widespread is the other aspect of the Janus-like image of Italy, and now of Pompeii, in Western literature: that of a region of eschatological anxiety, the home of the eerie and the sinister, '*cette fatale et criminelle Italie*' of Hugo's *Lucrèce Borgia*. Cazotte's *Le diable amoureux* and Mann's *Der Tod in Venedig*, Walpole's *The Castle of Otranto* and Gide's *Les caves du Vatican*, Tieck's *Pietro von Abano* and Bromfield's *Death in Monte Carlo* (set mainly in Venice) are among the many treatments of this particular view of Italy, which for sound historical reasons tends to be localized in the capital:

> '*Rome est le nid de la malice*
> *D'où sourdent tous les mauvais vices*'
>   (Guyot de Provins, *Bible satirique*)

and in Venice, a city which has elicited from its visitors reactions as schizophrenic as those of Alfred de Musset:

> '*Une heure est à Venise—heure des sérénades*
> *lorsque autour de Saint-Marc, sous les sombres arcades . . .*'

as well as

> ' *. . . Venise! ô perfide cité,*
> *A qui le ciel donna la fatale beauté . . .*'

In view of the spectacular fate visited upon the Campanian cities, it may seem odd that Pompeii should have had to wait for Bulwer-Lytton and Gautier (and Herculaneum, for Baudelaire's *Le jeune enchanteur*) in order to be demonized in its turn. Perhaps it was the very violence of that fate which retarded this process so long. The fact that Pompeii had already been so exemplarily punished in ancient times may have evened a moral account which in the case of Rome was to be presented again and again, from St Augustine through Luther and Milton to the present.

15 Detail of a fresco showing Mars and Venus, found at Pompeii. Museo Nazionale, Naples.

16a *Above* Mark Twain. British Museum, London.

16b *Below* Detail from the Battle of Alexander, a mosaic from the House of the Faun in Pompeii. Museo Nazionale, Naples.

The hero of the third narrative work to be considered here, Wilhelm Jensen's *Gradiva—ein pompejanisches Phantasiestück* (1904), is the archaeologist Norbert Hanold, who has brought back from a sojourn in Rome an ancient bas-relief which now hangs on the wall of his study, in a small town in Germany. It shows a young girl walking, and although not a valuable work of art it fascinates him because she moves in such odd fashion: 'The left foot had advanced, and the right . . . barely touched the ground with the tip of the toes, while sole and heel were raised almost vertically.' For some reason which he cannot fathom, Norbert connects her in his mind with Pompeii: could it be that she is shown crossing, in that characteristic gait of hers, a Pompeiian street? Had she, perhaps, been the daughter of a noble Campanian family devoted to the worship of the goddess Ceres? At any rate, this girl, to whom he had given the name of Gradiva or 'she who walks in splendour', pursues him even in his dreams. One night he sees her in ancient Pompeii, where he witnesses her death as she lies down on the steps leading to the Temple of Apollo and is slowly covered by falling ashes as by snow. The morning after this dream, he happens to be standing by the window of his apartment, watching people go by and idly listening to the song of a canary in the house across the street, when he sees a young woman who walks as Gradiva does on the bas-relief. He rushes down the stairs and into the street, but she has already been swallowed up by the crowd.

It is spring, and Norbert feels a seasonal yearning to take a trip. Being a well-to-do bachelor, he makes up his mind instantly to go south and into the sun. In the train he observes at close hand the behaviour of his many compatriots who also travel to Italy at this time of year, on their honeymoon; but in no case can he comprehend what 'he' sees in 'her', or 'she' in 'him'. These misanthropic notions are made more acute by an experience in the hotel in Rome, where he cannot help overhearing the conversation of the young couple in the room adjoining his own:

'My only Augustus.'
'My sweet Gretchen.'
'Now we have each other again.'
'Yes, at last we are alone again.'

'Must we go sightseeing again tomorrow?'

'We'll take a look at our Baedeker at breakfast, and see what is still to be done.'

'My only Augustus, I like you much better than the Apollo Belvedere.'

'And I have often thought, my sweet Gretchen, that you are more beautiful than the Capitoline Venus.'

'Is the volcano that we must climb near here?'

'No, I think we'll have to go by train a few hours in order to get there.'

'If it should begin to erupt just as we got on top, what would you do?'

'I would think only of saving you, and I would take you in my arms —like this!'

'Don't scratch yourself on that pin.'

'I can think of nothing better than to shed my blood for you.'

'My only Augustus.'

'My sweet Gretchen.'

With that, Rome is spoilt for Norbert. He goes to Naples, and, believing that the honeymoon couples will eventually end up in Capri, continues to Pompeii, where he takes a room at the Hotel Diomede. Having successfully evaded the honeymooners, he now discovers that their place is taken by the equally obnoxious and ubiquitous flies.

After a morning spent looking at the recent excavations, Norbert is ambling along the Street of Mercury, at noon when the other tourists have repaired to the hotel for lunch and a siesta, when he suddenly sees a familiar figure on the other side of the street; it is Gradiva, of course, who quickly disappears into the House of Meleager. He follows her into the garden and addresses her in Greek:

'Are you Atalanta, Jason's daughter, or are you a descendant of Meleager, the poet?'

Receiving no reply, he tries Latin: 'Was your father a distinguished Pompeiian of Roman origin?'

'If you wish to speak with me,' Gradiva replies with a smile, 'you must do so in German.'

Her voice somehow strikes him as familiar, and he asks her to lie down on the steps leading into the garden, as she had once done in his dream. But Gradiva only looks at him, as if he had made an unbe-coming request, and vanishes among the masonry. Unable to find a trace of her, Norbert returns to his room. At dinner, he examines the guests in his own hotel and the other one, the Hotel Suisse, without being able to find among them a woman who looks like Gradiva.

Hoping to see her again the next day, at noon and in the witching hour of the ancients, he picks a bouquet of asphodels which he takes with him to the House of Meleager. When she arrives, she asks where it was that he had seen her earlier, when she had lain down to sleep.

'In that night,' he replies, 'when you sat on the steps of the Temple of Apollo and let yourself be enveloped by the ashes from Vesuvius.'

He tells her that he had recognized her immediately from the bas-relief, adding that she would do him a great favour if she were to walk once more in the manner there shown. When she obliges him by taking a few steps, Norbert notices that she is wearing not sandals as on the bas-relief, but shoes of light-brown leather. He also discovers that she is called not Gradiva but Zoë, which takes him aback because this name, borne by a dead person, means 'life'.

Remarking that more fortunate girls are offered roses instead of asphodels, Gradiva accepts the bouquet and leaves with a promise to meet him again the following noon. Norbert picks up the sketchbook which she had forgotten, and sets out for a walk among the hills of Castellammare where he runs into an elderly gentleman, again of vaguely familiar aspect, who is hunting lizards with the aid of a noose fashioned out of a blade of grass. 'I don't suppose,' the stranger asks, 'that you are interested in *Faraglionensis*? You know, it seems very likely that they are found not only on the Faraglioni at Capri, but also on the mainland. The method suggested by Eimer, my colleague, is quite good. I have used it often, with much success. Please don't move . . .' Not knowing what to reply, the bewildered young man wants to return to his hotel, but loses his way and arrives not at the Diomede but at another inn, the Hotel Sole, of whose existence he had not known before. There, the manager talks him into buying a patina-covered antique brooch which had belonged to a girl whose remains, embraced by the skeleton of the lover into whose arms she had fled during the eruption, had been discovered in the course of the excavations. 'Had Gradiva-Zoë perhaps not been the only girl,' Norbert asks himself on his return to the Hotel Diomede, 'who had lain down to die in the presence of a man? Could the brooch possibly have been hers . . .?'

At dinner that evening in the hotel, he notices a newly-arrived couple at the next table. The woman has a rose in her dress, and Norbert, without really being aware of it, is agreeably surprised to find her there with her companion. When he retires for the night, he has another dream: Gradiva-Zoë is seated somewhere in the sun, making a noose out of a blade of grass and saying: 'Please don't move. My colleague is right, the method is quite good and she has used it with much success.'

Passing by the House of the Faun the next morning, Norbert feels a sudden compulsion to enter. As he turns a corner in the deserted building, he sees the couple from the hotel locked in an embrace. 'Another pair of lovers,' he says to himself, matter-of-factly, 'probably on their honeymoon.' Discreetly withdrawing from the scene, he makes his way to the House of Meleager, where Gradiva-Zoë accepts the brooch and the sketch-book which she had left behind the previous day. It being time for lunch, she even offers to share her meal with him: 'I feel as if we had broken bread together once before, two thousand years ago. Don't you remember?' Just then, one of the detested flies alights on her hand, and Norbert takes the chance for which he had been waiting: he touches her, the fly escapes, and he now knows that the girl is not a spirit but a flesh-and-blood woman. But her reaction to this familiarity is even more surprising, because she calls him by name: 'Norbert Hanold, you must be mad!' Before he can answer, the young couple from the House of the Faun enter. 'Zoë! You here, too?,' exclaims the woman, 'and also on your honeymoon? You haven't written me anything about it, you know.' While Norbert, by now totally confused, takes his leave with a mumbled excuse, Gradiva-Zoë tells her friend why she has come to Pompeii: not on her honeymoon but in order to look after her father, who had taken her along on condition that she would not disturb him on his lizard-hunting expeditions. Besides, she had consoled herself with the thought that she, too, would surely find something of interest in Pompeii.

Arranging to meet them later, she leaves the young couple to themselves and walks to the Villa of Diomedes, where Norbert had gone in order to collect his thoughts. It now turns out that his voyage to Pompeii had been unnecessary because he could as well have talked with Gradiva-Zoë back home in Germany, where she lived in the house with the canary, across the street from his own apartment. She is the daughter of Richard Bertgang, professor of zoology, and as a child had often played with Norbert, until the latter had taken up the study of archaeology and eventually lost all interest in the opposite sex, and indeed in all social activities. Now the scales finally fall from his eyes: 'Yes, now I see . . . no, you haven't changed at all . . . it is you, Zoë, my dear Zoë . . . how very odd!'

'That a person has to die in order to live again? For archaeologists, of course, this may be necessary.'

'No, I mean your name.'

'And what is so strange about that?'

'That Bertgang should mean the same as Gradiva: she who walks in splendour.'

She wants to return to the hotel now in order to look after her father, who customarily returns from the lizard-hunt at this hour. But a fly alights on her once more; in brushing it away, Norbert leans toward her face and ends by kissing her on the cheek. They decide to return to Pompeii on their own honeymoon, and walk to the hotel arm-in-arm, like any other Augustus and Gretchen. Before they can all go back to Germany, however, they have to prepare the professor for the impending loss of his daughter and hunting companion, a problem which Norbert proposes to solve by means of a ruse: he will cross over to Capri, catch a few lizards of the species *Faraglionensis*, and release them in Pompeii so that the old gentleman may catch them and contentedly leave for home.

In June 1906, Carl Gustav Jung, who had just declared his allegiance to the Psychoanalytical Movement, drew Sigmund Freud's attention to this story by pointing out to his mentor that it was a veritable treasury of psychoanalytical information. Freud read it and wrote his essay on *Der Wahn und die Träume in W. Jensens 'Gradiva'*, which among other things called forth the praise of the reviewer of the *Münchner Allgemeine Zeitung* who credited the author with literary gifts of such a high order that professional writers might well be envious of him.[6] In this earliest of all psychoanalytical interpretations of a literary text (a previous attempt at such an analysis, of C.F. Meyer's *Die Richterin*, having remained a fragment), Freud posits the thesis that a writer may intuitively gain psychological insights of a kind granted to the clinical investigator only after much labour, and that a parallel may therefore be said to exist between the former's poetic creation and the latter's scientific re-creation of the same material. In Freud's view, the motivation which Jensen furnishes for Norbert's delusion may be explained as follows:

> 'The erotic feelings in Norbert Hanold are repressed, and since his erotic drive knows and has known no object other than the Zoë Bertgang of his youth, his memories of her are forgotten. The ancient bas-relief awakens the slumbering eroticism in him and activates his childhood memories. On account of a resistance which he harbours against eroticism, these memories can become effective only in the unconscious mind. What follows is a struggle between the power of eroticism and the forces that are repressing it, a struggle which is "externalized" in the form of a delusion.'[7]

Since the raw material of this delusion consists of repressed childhood memories, Norbert's voyage follows a circular route: in escaping from the realization suggested in his first dream—that Gradiva is his contemporary, and in fact his neighbour—he unconsciously travels to the very place in which she will identify herself as just that. In the further course of his investigation, Freud identifies the various parallels which Jensen so meticulously built into his story, from the girl's gait, clothing, and physical appearance to the father's hieratic function (the service of the goddess Ceres in which Norbert imagined him engaged becomes a mere substitution for the equally exalted university service of the zoology professor Richard Bertgang). The canary and the flies, the asphodel as flower of death and the rose as flower of love, the sketch-book left behind as a pledge of return and the chase of the lizard (read: husband), even the play upon the Italian word for 'sun' (*il sole*, Hotel

Sole)—they all turn into coloured blocks, out of which the master builder of psychoanalysis here builds an admirably firm structure.

The labour performed by the girl, in acquiescing in Norbert's delusion that she is a Gradiva *rediviva*, is identical in nature to that performed by the clinical practitioner who brings to the surface those of his patient's feelings which find a symptomatic expression in *his* delusion; indeed, the doctor is even able in this instance to direct them back upon herself as upon the immediate cause of that delusion, a shortcut most unlikely to be available in real life where 'the physician has been a stranger, and must endeavour to become one again after the cure is finished; in many cases he does not know how to help the healed patient to apply in life his or her regained capacity for love'. The various stages of Norbert Hanold's cure may be traced in the development of individual motifs, such as the transformation of his dislike of honeymooning couples which turns to tolerance toward the couple in the hotel and ends with his self-identification with Augustus. The touching of Gradiva-Zoë's body when shooing away the flies thus represents a liberating repetition, on an adult level, of the childish games played with the neighbour's daughter, while the dream in which she lies down in a man's presence may be seen in the light of an anticipated marital relationship.

After its publication in May 1907, Freud sent the essay to Jensen, with the request of a critique. In his reply, the author acknowledged that Freud's analysis corresponded to his intention in writing the novel —not without taking care to add, however, that he considered his own poetic creation as the primary treatment of the motif, a claim which Freud had granted *a priori* in his essay. When he was later asked about the origin of the inspiration which had moved him to write *Gradiva*, Jensen mentioned that he had himself connected the bas-relief with Pompeii, and had even unsuccessfully searched for the original in the Museo Nazionale; only later had he been told that it was to be found in Rome (Jensen knew both cities, while Freud had been in Rome but not yet in Pompeii). In general, however, Jensen made it plain that he rejected any close identification of himself with the characters he had created, especially so after the psychoanalysts had begun to close in on him with interpretations of other works, the stories *Der rote Schirm* and *Im gotischen Hause* as well as the autobiographical *Fremdlinge unter den Menschen*. Freud, on his part, remained convinced that 'the continuation of the analysis would lead, through Jensen's childhood, to his most intimate erotic make-up'.[8]

The further ramifications of this correspondence in which Freud was engaged at a time when Jung, Graf, Stekel, Hitschmann, and still others had also begun to examine the possible applications of the new technique to literature, lead far afield from our subject. Nor do they have any bearing on the role which *Gradiva* played in the growth of psychoanalysis, a role which hinges on the fact that the story encouraged Freud to write an essay which deserves to be called epoch-making on a number of counts: as the first example of its kind and an exemplary demonstration both of the limitations of this approach and of its virtues and defects within these limitations; as a work which is uncommonly self-revelatory in regard to its author, to his essential modesty as a man and a scientist no less than to his combativeness (hence the many references to *Traumdeutung*, which had been published shortly before and for which Freud was viciously attacked); last but not least as a fruitful first confrontation of a psychoanalyst and a living writer still able to answer, or dismiss as the case may be, questions directed at him personally—in a word, a writer in a position to 'defend himself'. Jensen was already an old man at the time and seems never to have heard of Freud until the latter wrote to him; there is much to indicate that he did not realize the full significance of this encounter. The Psychoanalytical Movement, on the other hand, was still so much in its infancy that many of its early practitioners—in a reflex action which cries out for analysis—promptly bought copies of the bas-relief for the walls of their offices.

Here as in so many later instances, the limitations of the psychoanalytical interpretation of a literary work spring from the fact that objects of a different order of magnitude are measured as if no discrepancy existed between them. In reality, however, the little story composed in a few days by a second-rate author in his old age stands in no valid relation to this masterly essay by the greatest of all psychologists. And it is precisely because the calculation leaves no remainder, in striking contrast to practically all other such calculations either in literary criticism or in psychoanalysis, that one questions whether the sums so neatly added belong to the same category. (Freud himself, of course, who loved and knew so well his Shakespeare and Goethe, emphatically postulated at all times and in all relevant works—*Der Dichter und das Phantasieren, Das Motiv der Kästchenwahl, Eine Kindheitserinnerung aus 'Dichtung und Wahrheit'*, etc.—a fundamental difference between the acts of poetic and of scientific creation; indeed, he was particularly careful to stress this difference in his essay on *Gradiva*, in which yet another discipline plays a role: archaeology, a lifelong hobby of Freud's.)

The slight discomfort, then, which one feels on reading the essay is due neither to individual features of *Gradiva* itself (such as the circumstance, considered unlikely by Maiuri, that an expert like Norbert Hanold should have paid so much attention to an artistically inferior bas-relief)[9] nor to the acrobatics performed on the subject by later psychoanalysts: 'In some men,' one of the more humourous of these practitioners was to write, 'who feel a certain repugnance against the female body because it appears incomplete to them due to the lack of a penis (which children consider indispensable), homosexual tendencies may develop as a result of which the foot comes to pre-empt, as phallic symbol, all libidinous interest.'[10] Rather, the discomfort is rooted in that feeling of '*tant de bruit pour une omelette*' which occasionally overcomes one even in the presence of so good a cook as Freud. It is the stronger here as Thomas Mann was to write, only a few years later, a story which is infinitely superior to *Gradiva* and yet shares with it many of the motifs that fascinated Freud. In *Der Tod in Venedig*, too, a man suddenly departs for the south and realizes only much later that his real destination had been, from the beginning, not just Italy but a very specific locality in that country; there, too, we are shown the collapse of a personality which has hitherto been hermetically sealed off from its social surroundings, and the bursting forth of an erotic drive that had lain dormant and now comes to be fixed upon an unattainable object; there, too, the narrative is highlighted by dreams and underscored by *leitmotifs*. One cannot help wishing that *Death in Venice*, rather than *Gradiva*, had been available at a time when Freud had the inclination and leisure to examine contemporary writing from a psychoanalytical viewpoint.

We do no injustice to Freud if we point to a further weakness of his study on *Gradiva :* to the absence of any reference to Pompeiian literature as a whole. After all, many details which appealed to him as original and worthy of comment are not due to whatever inventive gifts Jensen may have possessed but inherent in the Pompeiian theme as such, beginning with that basic analogy between delving into a person's childhood and exploring the human past which has already been discussed in reference to Madame de Staël and could easily be shown to apply to several other writers as well. From the purely literary point of view, *Gradiva,* far from being original in concept and execution, is remarkable because it covers so much of the territory already staked out by Bulwer and Gautier—in the central plot of a love story set not only in Pompeii but very specifically localized in the Amphitheatre and the Forum, the Temple of Isis and the Street of Tombs, the House of the Faun and the Villa of Diomedes; in the fetishistic use made of parts of the body, which is less indicative of the respective author's psyche than of the fact that so many victims were found in Pompeii, often in positions which must have, so to speak, presented this particular motif on a platter to writers already attuned to the city and its strange fate; in the function assigned to dreams and superstitions, whether the witching hour begins at midnight as in the English and French works, or at noon as in the German one; in the adornment of the narrative with scholarly detail, and in much else. Nor can it be said that the three stories, here considered collectively as variations on a common theme, have exhausted the possibilities of the subject; indeed, one wonders why no one has yet written, in wholesome contrast to the speculations about Arbaces' skull, Arria's bosom, and Gradiva's foot, either a Pompeiian *Dinggedicht* after the fashion of Rilke's *Römische Fontäne* or a Pompeiian novel after the fashion of Graves' *I, Claudius.*

5

Pilgrims, Politicians, and Professors

'There are, unless you happened to be Toulouse-Lautrec, few
things in life less profitable than going to a brothel, unless,
Roderick reflected, it was going to a ruined brothel. This was a
whole street of ruined brothels. The houses had been built of
stone but it was necessary to use considerable imagination to
people them, least of all with delights. To him they resembled
at first rather a series of disjasked ovens, or, if one could
imagine pigpens made of bricks, pigpens, but with shelves and
niches, so that they seemed to have been made to accommodate
the consummations of some race of voluptuous dwarfs.
    "Roderick, do look, honey, here are the mills where the flour
was ground!—and the ovens, see, there's even a petrified loaf
of bread!"
    "*Si*, first bread, then wine, then woman on this-a street,"
Signor Salacci was nodding importantly. "First elements of
life, all symbolic!" '

MALCOLM LOWRY,
Present Estate of Pompeii

THE HISTORY of literature knows motifs and entire themes that have
been alternately treated by major writers and lain fallow, in periods
during which the great figures dealt with them either in passing or
not at all. We are familiar with this cyclical pattern of growth and
diminution, of waxing and waning in the literary heavens, from the
history of such archetypal personages as Medea and Faust, which spans
the centuries from Euripides to Anouilh and from Marlowe to Thomas
Mann. The same pattern applies to the archetypal city of Pompeii,
which, far from always occupying the centre of the stage in the works
in which it occurs, formed no more than an episode for some important
nineteenth-century writers. Before leaving the literary world for a
while and turning to politics and archaeology, we should briefly consider the role it played in the lives and works of three contemporaries
of Bulwer. In doing so we shall accompany the Pompeiian theme from
the peak it attained in the Romantic Age, into a valley from which it
has re-emerged only in recent years.

When he first visited Pompeii in 1845, Charles Dickens had yet to write *David Copperfield* and *Great Expectations*. One might nonetheless have been justified in expecting, of the man who had already published *The Pickwick Papers*, *Nicholas Nickleby*, *The Old Curiosity Shop*, and *Oliver Twist*, and seen, in France and the United States, a good bit of non-English life, more than one is offered in *Pictures from Italy*. Dickens, however, who was of course in essence a social critic and wrote only one or two historical novels, lacked not only classical erudition but that consuming interest in the past which is often engendered by such studies; moreover, the financial strain brought on by his mode of living, and occasionally travelling with family and household servants, left him no leisure to develop any deep under-standing of a foreign culture. Yet it is indicative of the man that he expressly warned the public, in 'The Reader's Passport' which forms an introduction to the book, not to look upon him as a source of original revelations in regard to Italy. In these, the most personal lines of the entire work, the author dissociates himself from those of his countrymen whose travel reports consisted of reflections on the Roman Church, of comments on the arts ('There is, probably, not a famous picture or statue in all Italy, but could be easily buried under a mountain of printed paper devoted to dissertations on it'), or 'any grave examination into the government or misgovernment of any portion of the country'. What remains is a description of Pompeii from which an excerpt may here be presented as a résumé not only of the collective impressions of former travellers but of those of many of Dickens' contemporaries—in short, as a sample of the work done by the capable journalist that Dickens had been in youth and became again in Italy:

'Stand at the bottom of the great market-place of Pompeii, and look up the silent streets, through the ruined temples of Jupiter and Isis, over the broken houses with their inmost sanctuaries open to the day, away to Mount Vesuvius, bright and snowy in the peaceful distance; and lose all count of time, and heed of other things, in the strange and melancholy sensation of seeing the Destroyed and the Destroyer making this quiet picture in the sun. Then, ramble on, and see, at every turn, the little familiar tokens of human habitation and everyday pursuits; the chafing of the bucket rope in the stone rim of the exhausted well; the track of carriage wheels in the pavement of the street; the marks of drinking vessels on the stone counter of the wineshop; the amphorae in private cellars, stored away so many hundred years ago, and undisturbed to this hour—all rendering the solitude and deadly lonesomeness of the place ten thousand times more solemn than if the volcano, in its fury, had swept the city from the earth and sunk it in the bottom of the sea.'

Despite his long friendship with Bulwer, and a second visit to the city undertaken 1853 in the company of the archaeologist Henry Layard, Dickens was not to return to this subject, which clearly meant no more to him than it had to countless other distracted tourists.

Among the public which attended the lectures given by Dickens on his second visit to New York was a man who had himself just returned from a long trip, and sat just then over the manuscript of a travel book which was to make him famous far beyond the borders of his own country. In a way, the account which Mark Twain gives of Pompeii in *The Innocents Abroad* (1869) is as unrewarding as that of the English novelist because it, too, tells very little about the author's personality or the state of the excavations. If we nevertheless quote a few lines from it, it is not because they add anything to our understanding of the future creator of *Huckleberry Finn* and *The Adventures of Tom Sawyer*, but because of their specifically American content. For the point of view from which this representative of a young and democratic nation regards Pompeii is not the traditional one of an archaeologist, poet, philosopher, or art historian, but that of a voting citizen, albeit a facetious one:

'. . . The sun shines as brightly down on old Pompeii today as it did when Christ was born in Bethlehem, and its streets are cleaner a hundred times than ever Pompeiian saw them in her prime. I know whereof I speak—for in the great, chief thoroughfares (Merchant Street and the Street of Fortune) have I not seen with my own eyes how for two hundred years at least the pavements were not repaired! —how ruts five and even ten inches deep were worn into the thick flagstones by the chariot-wheels of generations of swindled taxpayers? And do I not know by these signs that street commissioners of Pompeii never attended to their business, and that if they never mended the pavements they never cleaned them? And, besides, is it not the inborn nature of street commissioners to avoid their duty whenever they get a chance? I wish I knew the name of the last one that held office in Pompeii so that I could give him a blast. I speak with feeling on this subject, because I caught my foot in one of those ruts, and the sadness that came over me when I saw the first poor skeleton, with ashes and lava sticking to it, was tempered by the reflection that may be that party was the street commissioner.'

It is difficult to imagine a comment of this nature from the pen of a European writer. It bespeaks a concept of man as member of a community whose authorities are freely elected and can at any time be held accountable by the electorate—a pragmatic viewpoint, tempered in this instance with tolerance and a sense of humour, which adds to Pompeiian literature a new dimension and need not be couched in sceptical terms. When Mark Twain's compatriot James Jackson Jarvis, who later became an important collector and American vice-consul in Florence, came to Pompeii shortly after the middle of the century, he summarized his impressions in the significant sentence: 'The first thought that struck me was one of compliment to the departed "city fathers".'[1]

The reference to the days 'when Christ was born in Bethlehem' need not surprise us despite Mark Twain's rejection of much of the Christianity of his time. What other yardstick could he have applied, the young quasi-frontiersman who barely possessed the average learning of his time and came from a country that could look back on a history of two centuries at best? Nathaniel Parker Willis had similarly circumscribed the age of the Villa of Diomedes by stressing that it had last been inhabited 'while our Saviour was walking the earth', and William D. Howells later felt himself transported, by the train which conveyed him from Naples to Pompeii, from 'the nineteenth century [to] the first cycle of the Christian Era'.[2] This train, which the visitors had evidently not expected to find in a state as signally behind the times as the Kingdom of the Two Sicilies was in other and more important respects, seems to have impressed them beyond all measure. Jarvis comments on the 'shrieking fire horse' which took him to the excavations, and Herman Melville, of all people, found it necessary to observe, on a brief excursion to Pompeii undertaken in 1857, that 'R.R. same thing over the world'.[3] He was apparently unaware that Naples had got its first railway only two years after Paris, in the line to Granatello that had been inaugurated as early as 1839.

The frequency of such comments on the part of different American authors suggests that we have to do here with reactions which could in fairness be called 'typical' of the transatlantic tourists of the time. Yet in the aggregate, these visitors contributed little to Pompeiian lore, and it is no coincidence that three major American writers—Longfellow, Hawthorne, Henry James—should repeatedly have visited Naples without paying much attention to the excavations. The cities in which they resided and which were to play a significant role in their works were above all Rome, Florence, and Venice. It was there, not in Campania, that they hoped to find that for which they, pilgrims in the term's truest sense, had been adventurous enough to cross the ocean: the involvement in political activity which made Margaret Fuller such an ardent partisan of the Risorgimento; the particular brand of Romanticism cultivated by Washington Irving; that yearning for a synthesis of the Old World and the New which prompted James Fenimore Cooper to wish, in *Gleanings in Europe: Italy*, that it were possible to exchange for a year the populations of Rome and New York, so that 'the one party might partially awake from its dream of centuries [while] the other might discover that there is something valuable besides money'; the exposure to the international *haut monde* so dear to Henry James, and above all, that every-day contact with a viable and representative artistic tradition in which so many Americans gloried from the Pre-Raphaelites and Nazarenes to the Futurists. What is, perhaps, disappointing in the comments made on Campania by men like Mark Twain and J.J. Jarvis is not that they lacked that veneration for the historical past (a burden which many Europeans, too, carry only with ill grace and without benefit to themselves) without which a trip to Pompeii is only a nuisance, but that they made so little use of their superior topographical experience of the world. For example, both had already seen, by the time they visited Naples, the great volcanoes of the Hawaiian, or, as they were then called, the Sandwich

Islands; despite this advantage, their descriptions of Vesuvius are no more enlightening than those left by many central Europeans who had never before seen an active volcano. That such a comparative stance would have been well within the range of these authors is shown by two moderns: the Japanese Haruko Ichikawa opens the account of her visit to Naples with the monumental statement that 'Vesuvius is an exact replica of Mount Asama in Japan', while Malcolm Lowry takes the volcano's measure by calling it a 'Paricutín in reverse'.[4]

Although he suffered, in the eyes of posterity, a greater diminution in stature than Dickens or Mark Twain, Alexandre Dumas *père* was once considered the leading novelist of the nineteenth century. One of his earliest works is *Le Corricolo* (1845), part of the *Impressions de voyage*. It consists of a series of lively episodes in the best—or worst— Dumas style: folk scenes replete with clanking swords, passionate glances from fiery black eyes, and *bel canto* (it was in the 1840s that 'Santa Lucia' set out to conquer the concert hall)—*capa y espada* such as one finds elsewhere in the travel literature of the period, but with an admixture of humour as in the anecdote about the Bey of Algiers, who while staying at the fashionable Hotel Vittoria sent his bodyguard Mustapha to the kitchen with orders to borrow a long knife. When asked why it had to be so long, he replied: 'So that I can cut off Ali's head' [Ali, a eunuch, had been caught at some minor misdemeanour or other]. The manager quickly sent word to Del Carretto, the Minister of Police, who told the honoured guest that this was not the way such things are done in the Hotel Vittoria—whereupon the disappointed Bey departed the next morning in search of a land 'where a man can do with his property as he wishes'. Elsewhere in the book, the account of the Villa of Diomedes and other Pompeiian monuments is prefaced by a remark which characterizes the whole work: 'Let the reader be at his ease, for we have no intention of taking him along on an excursion into the family life [of the ancients]. We shall look at three or four of the more important buildings, visit this or that shop, walk past a temple, cross the forum, stroll through a theatre, read a few inscriptions, *et ce sera tout*.' The author continues to mock scholarly pedantry in a passage on the 'Battle of Alexander', in which he details the arguments advanced by the experts for the interpretation of the great mosaic; does it really depict Alexander and Darius at Arbela or Issus, or does it represent quite different military leaders and engagements, Marathon, perhaps, or Platea, or Pharsalus, or even the battle which Drusus fought at Lyons against the Gauls? In contrasting these varied views with one another, Dumas cites the ancients at every juncture; we may assume, in view of the speed with which he wrote even then and the fact that he liked to turn out his works assembly line-fashion with many assistants, that this documentation was provided by his Neapolitan collaborator, Pier Angelo Fiorentino. All in all, then, *Le Corricolo* is an entertaining book, but of so little specific weight that it would scarcely be worth bothering about if the author's voyage of 1835, on which it is based, had not in turn been followed by a far more significant Pompeiian experience.

Dumas' great days coincided with the reign of Louis-Philippe, the Citizen King. With *Henri III et sa cour, Antony, Le Tour de Nesle,* and other plays he had become a standard bearer of Romanticism along with Hugo and Lamartine, a position which he strengthened with the publication of *Les trois mousquetaires* and *Le comte de Monte-Cristo* in 1844-45. Then came the Revolution of 1848 with Louis-Philippe's abdication, the *coup d'état* of 1852 and Hugo's exile, and that change in literary fashion which was rung in by the fiasco of *Les burgraves* and confirmed by the success of *Madame Bovary*. Within a few years, Dumas' standing so declined that he remained only a shadow of his former self—a *boulevardier* who held court in cafés, wrote ever faster in order to keep pace with his steadily mounting debts, kept company with ladies young enough to be his daughters, and was in fact surpassed in fame by his own son. By 1859, it seemed to him time to turn his back on the fickle Parisian public and to restore his self-confidence by means of a sea journey to the Levant, to the Holy Land and to Egypt where his father, the general, had so distinguished himself some sixty years before. Dumas accordingly had a yacht built in Marseilles, baptized it the *Emma* and put to sea, in early 1860, with a hired crew and the actress Emilie Cordier (dressed, for the occasion, in a sailor suit). The first lap of the journey took them past the Chateau d'If and on into Genoa, which they found in a frenzy of excitement on account of the

11

recent departure of Garibaldi and his Thousand. Dumas, who had already made the patriot's acquaintance and so admired him that he eventually edited his autobiography, decided to let the Levant go and to follow Garibaldi to Sicily instead. There he was received with open arms, established in the former Bourbon governor's palace, and allowed to accompany as a war correspondent General Türr's expedition into the interior; Mademoiselle Cordier, to be sure, whose advanced state of pregnancy could no longer be disguised as a jolly sailor's *embonpoint*, had to remain behind in Palermo. After a series of adventures worthy of a d'Artagnan aged fifty-eight, he returned aboard the *Emma*, sailed up into the Gulf of Salerno where he accepted, dressed in a fantastic uniform of his own design, the capitulation of an enemy regiment, and eventually participated in the negotiations which led to the surrender of the capital. As a reward for his many services to the Expedition of the Thousand, as arms smuggler and propagandist, he was appointed director of the Campanian excavations and given an official residence in a decree published on September 14, 1860:

> '*M. Dumas est autorisé à occuper, d'ici à un an, le petit palais Chiatamone, en sa qualité de directeur des fouilles et musées.*
>
> > G. Garibaldi'

After establishing his household, he set about studying sketches and maps of the buried cities, which he intended to restore to the sun with the aid of French archaeologists called in from Paris and a detachment of engineering troops. But this dream did not last beyond the few days in which the leader of the Red Shirts still exercised dictatorial powers. The King of Sardinia, Victor Emanuel II, had his hands full with Garibaldi and had no intention whatever of entrusting to a writer, and a foreign one at that, any part of the Sardinian, or as it became the Royal Italian, Army. The Neapolitans, too, wanted to be left in peace, and when it was bruited about that Dumas had distributed arms— Francis II having entrenched himself in the fortress of Gaeta, the war was to continue until well into the following year—and used the excavations for elaborate receptions reminiscent of those given, in more peaceful days, by the deposed King's uncle, Leopold Count of Syracuse, they demonstrated so vehemently before the gates one evening that Dumas noticed it and looked up from his papers: 'Another demonstration? Against whom? Against what? What more do they want? Don't they have their *Italia una?*' But the shouts could no longer be ignored: 'Away with Dumas! *Fuori straniero!* Into the sea with him!' The tumult subsided only when troops were called out and dispersed the crowd at bayonet point. Tactful beyond the call of duty, the colonel remarked that the Neapolitan mob had not changed since the days of Masaniello; but the despondent novelist only replied: 'I have become accustomed to the ingratitude of France, but I had not expected that of the Italians.'

Although the cup of his bitterness ran over when Emilie left him after being delivered of a daughter, Dumas remained in Naples until 1864, publishing a newspaper, writing *causeries* for the Paris press, and occasionally visiting Pompeii. But the interlude of the author who had wanted not to describe but to excavate the city, was finished once and for all.

At the risk of running ahead by a few decades of the chronological sequence of events, mention should here be made of the attempt made by another outsider to take the work out of the natives' indolent hands and to speed it up through the importation of foreign experts. In the course of this endeavour, long-neglected Herculaneum joined its sister city in the political limelight, as it had during the Napoleonic period and in the heyday of the *Risorgimento*.

Shortly after the turn of the century, the British archaeologist Charles Waldstein became convinced that the excavation and restoration of Herculaneum would be more rewarding than that of Pompeii. The Greek element, more creative culturally than the Italic, had been stronger there than in largely Osco-Samnite Pompeii, and the discovery of the papyri as well as the comparative scarcity of shops and other business premises seemed to indicate that intellectual life had blossomed more richly in the smaller city; the dried mud had sealed off the houses of Herculaneum hermetically, and preserved them better than the porous mixture of earth and lapilli under which Pompeii had come to rest (so that bronzes from Herculaneum acquired a dark-hued patina while the Pompeiian ones are light-green and partially oxydized); moreover, the small section of Herculaneum excavated during the past century-and-a-half had yielded, per cubic yard, more numerous and more valuable works of art than any corresponding part of Pompeii (a disproportion since equalled by the discoveries of more recent years). For these reasons and because archaeological working conditions were more favourable in Pompeii, where it was sometimes sufficient to dig horizontally without sinking deep shafts, those excavations had progressed so much faster that Pompeii had gained a lead, as it were, over Herculaneum, which now had to draw even. Given the financial burdens inherent in large-scale archaeological work, burdens which no individual nation could be expected to shoulder, Waldstein proposed to entrust the excavation of Herculaneum to an International Commission made up of experts and leading citizens of the various participating countries, which would collect, from public and private sources, the necessary sums (he reckoned in terms of an annual budget of £40,000).

Some form of supranational collaboration, Waldstein thought, was called for also because it alone could guarantee the adoption of the most recent advances in tunnelling and other aspects of civil engineering and thus free archaeology from the methodological rigidity in which it found itself, in contrast to other sciences which had made much greater strides in point of technology; last but not least, it would tend to mitigate the 'malevolent recrudescence' of chauvinism in the modern world. The moral obligation which the western nations had incurred, in the course of history, toward Italy as the oldest son of that family could now be redeemed if, for example, England and the United States, which possessed within their borders no appreciable remnants of ancient cultures, were to contribute a little of their financial strength and technical know-how to the task of restoring that portion of the common cultural heritage from antiquity that still rested in Italian soil. His own experience as Director of the American School of Archaeology in Athens and Slade Professor of Fine Art at Cambridge had convinced him of the feasibility of international collaboration in these matters. Waldstein therefore proposed, in late 1903, the establishment of a national committee in each participating country, under the honorary presidency of the respective head of state. The International Commission could then constitute itself, in Rome and under the patronage of the King of Italy, from among the delegates sent by the various national bodies. It would be the duty of this Commission, to which the Italian Minister of Public Instruction as well as the Mayor of Naples should belong *ex officio*, to select the archaeologists, engineers, art historians, and other experts charged with the actual work, to act as a final court of appeal in all disputes, to undertake the publication of the findings by means of weekly (!) reports published in several languages, and to take charge of the finances.

Since the implementation of this ambitious project depended above all on the good will of the exalted personages to whom he intended to offer the presidency of the national committees, Waldstein now began to travel from capital to capital in order to 'sell' his project in person. Having first enlisted the support of his own sovereign, Edward VII, he went to Italy in order to secure an expert opinion on the technical feasibility of the project as well as the permission to excavate on the actual site; he received assurances on both points, from the seismologist Giuseppe Mercalli and the municipality of Resina, respectively. After an equally heartening interview with the Italian Minister of Public Instruction (Vittorio Emanuele Orlando, the later Prime Minister and the smallest of the Big Four of Versailles), Waldstein laid his plan before the public at large by means of an announcement in *The Times* of April 23, 1904. In the course of his further travels and of the correspondence into which he now entered with Secretary of State John Hay, French Minister of Public Instruction Jean Chaumié, German Chancellor Bernhard v. Bülow, and other luminaries of this calibre, he obtained promises from Presidents Theodore Roosevelt and Emile François Loubet, Kaiser Wilhelm II, and King Oscar II of Sweden that they would act as honorary presidents of the respective national committees. Only Victor Emanuel III of Italy, on whose consent everything depended, appeared strangely hesitant, declaring that as a constitutional monarch he was bound to consult his ministers before committing himself; and these ministers, from Giolitti down, were in turn reluctant to make a recommendation without the advice of the country's leading archaeologists, men who had suddenly become extraordinarily difficult to contact. In December 1904, Waldstein laid the entire scheme before the Royal Society and departed on a fundraising trip to the United States.

The Italian ambassador to the Court of St James, the aptly named Signor Panza, had attended Waldstein's lecture and undertaken the distribution of the passes which would admit representatives of the Italian press to that function. Due to an oversight or whatever, these passes did not get into the reporters' hands until the day *after* the event, with the result that these men, the London correspondents of the leading Italian dailies, had to rely on their English colleagues for information about the lecture. The London papers had, however, left out, as of little interest to their own readers, the one item which mattered in this connection: the speaker's assurances, so vital for the preservation of Italian *amour-propre*, that from the king to the lowliest museum guard, Italian authorities were to be put in charge of administering the project.

The omission was to have fatal consequences because it caused the Italian government to disassociate itself from the project, by means of a series of artfully edited telegrams and other news releases which culminated in a declaration to the effect that no concrete proposals had ever been submitted to Rome, and that the government therefore wished to preserve for itself complete freedom of action. At the very same time as the indefatigable archaeologist thought that he had gained firm ground under his feet after interviews with Theodore Roosevelt in the White House and J. Pierpont Morgan in Wall Street, that ground was being pulled out from under him by the Italian government, in so abrupt a fashion that he feared for his good name: 'I beg you to vindicate my honour publicly before Tuesday,' he cabled Orlando on 1 January 1905, 'so that I may not stand before the world as a lying imposter—*bugiardo impostore*.'[5] Although it was eventually forthcoming, this vindication was granted so slowly and grudgingly as to be in effect useless; Waldstein returned to Europe a gentleman, to be sure, but also as a man who had failed, the more so as further reports had meanwhile spread the rumour that the patronage of the International Commission was to be offered not to Victor Emanuel but to Theodore Roosevelt, whereupon the Italian government withdrew its support completely. Negotiations continued for some time yet, but the public soon lost interest, and the plan to excavate Herculaneum under the direction of a supranational authority was formally laid to rest in early 1907, when it was announced in Rome that the city was to be restored to the light under exclusively Italian auspices.

The time was not yet ripe for large-scale archaeological collaboration on an international level; it has only come in our days, with the preservation of the Abu Simbel monuments under UNESCO direction. Waldstein had no such inter-governmental scaffolding to support his project, and in improvising one probably made a mistake when he began with the roof, with anointed and elected heads of state, and neglected to build a foundation of continuing public interest kept alive by a power which would not now be underestimated by even the most inexperienced scholar: the press. This miscalculation, in turn, may reflect his own personality, for he was not an entrepreneurial type but a gentleman-scholar. Although defeated in the end by the archaeological and journalistic establishment of the day, Waldstein at least had the consolation of having lived through some memorable hours, like that September evening in 1904 when he attended a command dinner at the court of Wilhelm II: 'After dinner, the emperor had the Cambridge professor summoned to his presence, in order to be informed about the details of the proposed excavation of Herculaneum. Agreeing immediately with Waldstein's plan, the Emperor said: "Let us do this right now. I will act as honorary president of the German committee, and one of my princes shall have the active chairmanship." . . . The emperor had heard that the professor was a fine horseman, and jokingly observed, referring to certain fox hunts in which Waldstein was said to have taken part: "So you are the professor who rides to hounds?"—"Indeed I am, Your Majesty," replied Waldstein, "but I trust it does not reflect on my scholarship," whereupon the Kaiser said: "On the contrary, I wish my professors did likewise!" '⁶

If Waldstein failed despite his energy and the support of his crowned patrons, it was in part because archaeological work in Campania had made significant advances since the unification of Italy. The excavations were no longer being carried out as primitively as Waldstein had intimated, and the men in charge were accordingly far less vulnerable to his criticism than their predecessors had been to that of Winckelmann. With the appointment of Giuseppe Fiorelli as Director of the Museum and Excavations, the work had for the first time been entrusted to a man who possessed not only the requisite talents and training but the full confidence of the authorities—now of the Italian government, transferred from Turin to Florence, and thence to Rome in 1870. Fiorelli, a native of Naples, had made his name as a young man with a publication on the financial practices of the ancients, and when imprisoned in 1848 on account of his Liberal sympathies used the enforced idleness in order to complete a *Pompeianarum antiquitatum historia*. Upon being released, he was recommended to the brother of King Ferdinand II, the progressively inclined Leopold, Count of Syracuse, who employed the young archaeologist as his secretary, thereby protecting him from further prosecution. After the accession to the throne of his nephew, Francis II, Leopold redoubled his efforts to forestall the threatening dissolution of the ruling dynasty, by re-orienting Neapolitan policy in such a manner that it would follow the trend of the times rather than running counter to it. Instead of attempting to sabotage all endeavours to unite Italy under the House of Savoy, he thought, the Two Sicilies should anticipate these moves and take the wind out of Cavour's sails. Had the cabinet followed this advice the Bourbons might possibly have maintained their influence in a united Italy, much as the Bavarian Wittelsbachs preserved theirs in Bismarck's *Reich*. As it was, the inexperienced young monarch, whose father had already forfeited all sympathies in his role as *Re Bomba*, stuck to the repressive policy which was to cost him the throne. At the very last moment, when Garibaldi had already occupied Sicily and gained a foothold in Calabria, Leopold charged his secretary with the drafting of a letter in which he enjoined his royal cousin to abdicate, for the sake of the country's future, a throne which he could not possibly hope to occupy much longer: '. . . With these words, Sire, I fulfill the sacred duty imposed by my experience, and I pray to God that He enlighten you and make you worthy of His blessings. From Your Majesty's most affectionate uncle Leopold, Count of Syracuse.'[7]

Issued on August 24, 1860, this proclamation hastened the downfall of the Bourbon dynasty, now openly divided against itself, and there-with the demise of that Kingdom of the Two Sicilies under whose aegis the excavation of the Campanian cities had until then taken place.

As author of the proclamation, Fiorelli was assured of the gratitude of Victor Emanuel II, the *Re Galantuomo* with the gigantic moustache, the more so as this first ruler of modern Italy had long considered the restoration of Pompeii and Herculaneum as one of the most urgent tasks to be shouldered by the new state. Having already been appointed, in 1864, to the chair of archaeology at the University of Naples, Fiorelli was now given charge of the excavations and eventually made a Senator of the Realm and Director-General of Arts and Antiquities for all Italy. During his eleven years in Pompeii he introduced the methods and practices which, refined by his successors (the professors Michele Ruggiero, Giulio de Petra, and in our century chiefly Amedeo Maiuri and Alfonso de Franciscis), are still being followed today.

First of all, the city was divided into *regiones* and *insulae*, and instead of being treated as an inexhaustible source of supply for museums it was looked upon as a memorial site for the entire sweep of ancient life including its domestic, commercial, and otherwise non-artistic dimensions. The '*Giornale degli scavi*' or logbook of the excavations was accordingly transformed from a dynastic into a scientific publication, from a court circular commemorating this or that royal visit into a business-like record of what had been found when and where. Instead of digging out buildings at random, entire *insulae* or city blocks were now opened up one at a time, and the debris removed by means of a specially constructed narrow-gauge railway. Digging was no longer done horizontally, i.e., sideways from the street into the houses (which had often caused their roofs, still weighed down with earth and ashes, to collapse upon the hapless workmen), but vertically, through the roof downwards into the various rooms. When Fiorelli received a message one day that another group of bodies had just been discovered, he gave orders to stop the work immediately, went to the locality in person, and carefully poured a special plaster of Paris-like solution into the hollow space left by the flesh which had rotted away so many centuries ago. When it had dried a few days later, the material was found to have preserved the outline of the body and in some cases even the imprint of the victim's clothing and his or her facial expression. Ingenious as the method was and is, it can be used to advantage only in the case of victims who had been overwhelmed by mud which had dried before the fleshy parts had decayed; where the person had asphyxiated in an hermetically enclosed space, only the bones remained, whose salvage entailed braving the mephitic gases which had preserved their virulence through all these centuries. A sizeable number of bodies have been preserved by this method since Fiorelli first adopted it on the four victims found in the *Vico degli scheletri* or 'Skeletons' Way' of Pompeii: that of the dog which had climbed as high as its chain would allow on the heap of ashes which relentlessly grew under its feet, that afternoon of August 24, 79 in the house of the fuller and dry-cleaner Vesonius Primus; the young girl and the huge man whose forms are still to be seen in the little museum near the Marine Gate; and the two women, probably mother and daughter, who had sought refuge, in their death throes, in each other's arms. Although the preservation of skeletal remains had until then been a matter of chance as with Arria's hip and bosom, the new method could be employed only in Pompeii because Herculaneum had a much smaller population and is still largely unexplored.

Among the most important of the findings made by Fiorelli and his successors has been the discovery (1875) of an iron-sheathed chest containing some of the wax-covered wooden tablets used by the ancients for their business transactions, and recording, in this case, receipts dated from the years A.D. 65–70; that of the country estate of Boscoreale (1895) with its silver treasure, now in the Louvre, and the oil and wine presses which suggest that even patrician premises had often been turned into a source of income through being used as outlets for the sale of homegrown produce and products; that of the House of the Vettii (1896), next to the House of the Faun probably the most famous of all private dwellings in Pompeii, and of the Villa of the Mysteries (1909–10 and 1929–30) with its paintings; that of the statue of the Ephebus, and that of the Narcissus of which an identical copy was found in France, so that the possibility of a standardized or serial manufacture of art objects in antiquity cannot be dismissed; that of the House of the Menander (1930), with a further collection of silverware and jewelry; shortly before the Second World War, that of the *palaestra*, with almost one hundred bodies and the magic square, as well as the so-called crucifix and *prie-Dieu* of Herculaneum; that of the ivory statuette of the Indian love goddess Lakshmi (taken to be an indication of the existence of a trade route to the Orient), and in the winter of 1942–43, of the *bucchero* vessels under the Temple of Apollo, which appears to support the theory of an Etruscan interregnum in Pompeii about the year 500 B.C.

Keeping pace with these discoveries, which can be sketched here only in barest outline, has been the preservation and maintenance of what had been and is being brought to light. Frescoes are now only protected against the climate and otherwise left untouched, so that they may continue to fulfill their original decorative and perspective function. Coloured stucco decorations have been similarly covered with glass panes, while earth and ashes were carefully sifted and sieved wherever the remains of cloth or a wooden box suggested the possibility that jewelry or other valuables may once have been kept in that place. Ever since the beginning of Maiuri's term of office, bushes and flowers have been planted in the gardens, after the horticultural experts had learned to identify, from the carbonized remains of their roots and stems, the particular species that had once grown there. These and many other restorative measures had to be carried out under trying conditions, in the face of further eruptions of Vesuvius and under the threat of destruction in World War II, in which the city barely escaped being obliterated for the second time (sixty cases with gold, silver, and glass objects which had been stored in Monte Cassino as late as June 1943, were removed from the abbey in the nick of time; two guns emplaced near the Tower of Mercury were never fired in earnest, and the air attacks of September 1943, during which some 150 bombs had been dropped on the city, were called off when it turned out that the Germans had not taken up position in the *scavi nuovi* after all, although the corrugated tin roofs of that part of the excavations may indeed have resembled military installations from the air). Moreover, the abuses which had so long bedeviled the work have been largely eliminated. Thefts are rare nowadays, and the festivities that used to be arranged on the site under the Bourbons, and even under Mussolini as late as 1940 when the Nazi Minister Bernard Rust was entertained in the *sala triclinense* of the House of the Menander, are likewise a thing of the past. Some three-fifths of Pompeii have thus been restored, and it need not be long before the entire city will have been excavated. The science of archaeology which Winckelmann had observed in its infancy has long ago matured in Campania as elsewhere, and as one looks back on its coming of age, it is not without a sense of wonder that one recalls the many instances of bungling which marked this process: 'The guide followed us with a large pail of water,' a visitor noted less than two hundred years ago, 'and whenever we entered a room that contained paintings, he would splash water on the dusty walls so that the . . . frescoes suddenly emerged as bright and beautiful as if they had been painted yesterday.'[8]

In the first century of the excavation of Pompeii, literature had far outrun archaeology; during the past hundred years, this balance has been redressed. The topic had lost the gloss of novelty, and although the city was described again and again, it was usually done in terms of a repetition of commonplaces. Hippolyte Taine, Massimo d'Azeglio, Miguel de Unamuno and many others paid it a perfunctory tribute in the spirit of that '*nihil novum sub sole*' of which Vicente Blasco-Ibáñez felt himself reminded there.[9] Even details that were clearly wrong were so faithfully transmitted from generation to generation that over a hundred years after the excavations had first begun, a much-used German reference work listed the population of ancient Pompeii as 40,000 and that of Herculaneum as 'in excess of 100,000'.[10] If the subject had formerly appealed particularly to the great, to Goethe and Schiller, Madame de Staël and Lamartine, Shelley and Leopardi, it was now almost totally neglected by men like Turgenev and Ibsen, Rilke and Rolland, Henry James and Thomas Mann—travellers all, and at one time or another residents of Italy. The element of exoticism and adventure which had once lured so many foreigners to southern Italy had disappeared with the advent of the railway and the steamer; with the country's unification there had also ended the various endeavours, of non-Italians as well as natives, to help that nation find a political organization adequate to its needs, and hence to stress, often with specific reference to Pompeii, the appalling contrast between its former grandeur and present misery; and the social and other questions of the turn of the century were even further removed from the

Campanian cities. Whether they were concerned about the perils of industrialization or the position of woman in modern society or the emergence of transatlantic concepts and practices in European life or the triumph of experimental science, men did not dream of going to Pompeii when they sought solutions to these and other problems of the age.

One might be tempted, then, to consider as closed the development of a literary tradition which could properly be called Pompeiian—if the fire had not continued to smolder under the ashes and, more importantly, if our existential situation had not so changed in recent years that everything hitherto written about Pompeii may well turn out to have been but a prologue. For what we have before us is not only a revival of this motif in modern poetry (Loerke's *Pompejanischer Abend*, Del Valle's *A Pompeya*, Montale's *Sarcofaghi*), drama (Ödön v. Horváth's *Pompeji*), and belles-lettres (Malaparte's *La pelle*, Peyrefitte's *Le gardien de Pompéi*), but its occurrence in the works of two authors who were not epigones of the past but prophets of the future.

Felix Hartlaub, with Borchert perhaps the most gifted among the young German writers destroyed by World War II, had visited the excavations already as a student. The sketch of the Expressionist story *Daedalus gründet Cumae* and the *novella Parthenope* (1934) show a familiarity with the Campanian landscape which would surely have borne further fruit in the planned work about the inscription SODOMA GOMORA. That the city's fate had become a viable symbol to Hartlaub is also apparent from his war diary, the *Tagebuch aus dem Kriege* with its description of a French government building in which desks, shelves, archives, etc. still look as they had a year earlier, when the ministry had been hurriedly deserted by its occupants:

'Hundreds of rooms along the large corridor. Every door broken open, every cupboard and desk rifled. The drawers stick out pitifully from the pompous "*bureaux d'acajou*". Streams of letters have flown over onto the floor, the platoon leafs through photo albums, dust lies already half a finger thick. Pompeiian effects: all calendars indicate June 14, 1940 . . .'[11]

The parallel between Pompeii and Paris, between the city struck down in life and that ripe unto death, had already been glimpsed by Melville and others gifted with a sharp eye for the cracks in the universe. It is restated by Hartlaub in the designation *città morta*, here applied to the fallen French capital with its 'government quarters so strangely swept empty,' and brings to mind the exclamation 'The City of the Dead! the City of the Dead!' which Sir Walter Scott had kept repeating to himself on being led through Pompeii. There is little doubt that Hartlaub, had he lived, would have returned after the war to Pompeii, to this apocalyptic theme which he had already calibrated for himself as an artist in the sketch *Terminus und die Laren sterben* and as a writer in the drama *Der verlorene Gott*.

Although he also died young, the Anglo-Canadian Malcolm Lowry left behind an opus of sufficient size and distinction to warrant the belief that he will not soon be forgotten. In the short story *Present Estate of Pompeii*, the Canadian Roderick McGregor Fairhaven arrives in Pompeii by train, with his young wife who enjoys every moment of their European trip. Since the weather is menacing anyway, he wants to remain in the Restaurant Vesuvius in which they are taking their lunch, in order to get drunk quietly: 'Inside the restaurant during the thunderstorm, there was one moment of pure happiness within the dark inner room when it started to rain. "Now thank God I don't have to see the ruins," Roderick thought.' In the end, however, he has to put up with the inevitable tour, with his wife and a guide; but the thoughts and sensations which pass through his mind on this humdrum occasion have nothing in common with the precious sentimentalities so often uttered on this spot. They are insights into the human condition as such, and in reading a few samples one wonders why we had to wait from the Romantic Age until the year 1948 before Pompeii once more brought forth such reflections: ' "Pompeii," Tansy was reading aloud from her guidebook—as now thank God it started to rain again—"an old Oscan town dating from the sixth century B.C., which had adopted the Greek culture, lay in the rich and fertile Campania Felix close to the sea, possessing moreover a busy harbour . . ."

"I know . . . it exported fish sauce and millstones . . . But I was thinking—" Roderick brought out his pipe—"that I've read little about the malaise of travellers, even the sense of tragedy that must come over them sometimes at their lack of relation to their environment."

"—what?"

"The traveller has worked long hours and exchanged good money for this. And what is this? This, pre-eminently, is where you don't belong. It is some great ruin that brings upon you this migraine of alienation—and almost inescapably these days there seems a ruin of some kind involved—but it is also something that slips through the hands of your mind, as it were, and that, seen without seeing, you can make nothing of: and behind you, thousands of miles away, it is as if you could hear your own real life plunging to its doom."

"Oh for God's sake, Roddy . . .!"

* * *

He reached in his pocket for some matches and a news clipping fluttered out.

"Is that Dad's latest news report flying away?" Tansy said.

Roderick's father-in-law, who was a boatbuilder in British Columbia, near Vancouver, scarcely ever wrote his daughter at all and his correspondence with Roderick consisted of clippings from newspapers . . . The enclosure Roderick had received at the American Express in Naples this morning was . . . half a page, mostly given over to advertisements . . . and crowned by the gigantic headline: OIL! OIL! OIL! . . . At first Roderick thought this was an ironic reference to their own small speculation, which had so astonishingly paid off. Then he saw the item the old man had marked: a small 'filler' which apparently had nothing to do with British Columbia at all and ran:

SCARED TO DEATH

In Arizona, a 1,000-acre forest of junipers suddenly withered and died. Foresters are unable to explain it, but the Indians say the trees died of fear but they are not in agreement as to what caused the fright.

* * *

Until a man has built . . . a house with his own hands, Roderick thought, he may feel a sense of inferiority before such things as Greek columns. But if he happens to have helped build so much as a summer shack upon the beach he will not feel inferiority, even if he does not understand in the aggregate the entire meaning of a Doric temple . . .

Ridiculous and far-fetched though it might sound, what he had been thinking gave Roderick, finally, a certain kinship with the builders of Pompeii . . . But these Pompeiians—what had they built for? What was this instinct that made man herd together like partridges, like sardines in tomato paste, this cowardly dependence on the presence of others? Suddenly he thought he knew what was wrong. This—in Pompeii, in Naples—this had happened to him, to Roderick McGregor Fairhaven, the visitor from Ultima Thule. What it amounted to was a feeling that there was not going to be time. Did you want to harrow yourself looking at what had been only temporarily spared, at what was finally doomed? And Roderick could not help but wonder whether man too was not beginning to stand, in some profound inexplicable sense, fundamentally in some such imperfect or dislocated relation to his environment as he. Man once stood at the centre of the universe, as Elizabethan poets stood at the centre of the world.—But the difference between the man-made ruins and the ruins of Pompeii was that the man-made ones had not for the most part been found worth preserving, or had been carried away. Had some precious part of man been carried away with the ruins? Partly it was as if man built with ruin in view . . . See Naples and die!'

The dialogue between husband and wife talking past one another is as new in Pompeiian literature as the figure of the 'dislocated' modern traveller who, surfeited with culture and joylessly rushing from place to place, can no more escape his doom than can an animal caught in the morass where its every movement only serves to imprison it the more irreversibly. Equally new is the raising of the obligatory *cicerone* to autonomous stature, to a guide into the nether regions, to a Hermes Psychopompos. These existential variations of the Pompeiian motif, of that so strangely modulated *memento mori*, are here achieved without forfeiting the cultural concerns evoked by a visit to this locality, for this writer knows his Volney and Lamartine and speaks not by chance of the 'desolation that comes to one eternally wading through the poem of *The Waste Land* without understanding it.'

No one can yet determine the place that will eventually be assigned to Malcolm Lowry in the literary history of the twentieth century. No one can even say with any certainty that such a history will ever be written; for we have no way of telling whether the world as we know it is irrevocably headed for disaster, or whether those will turn out to have been right who believe in a future in which even the stars will become accessible to us. This much is certain: that we, in contrast to all generations that have gone before us, must live with the knowledge that we may be swept from the face of the earth by a fate beyond all known violence—obliterated not as individuals, not as members of a family or social group, not as citizens of this or that country, but simply as human beings. It is more than likely that this truly 'Pompeiian' condition of modern man will eventually be painted in the same colours in which the writers of the past have depicted the life, death, and rebirth of this city.

Notes and Bibliography

Chapter 1

Notes

1 *Silvae*, V, 3, 164. In epigram No. IV, 44, Martial speaks of *Veneris sedes*.
2 *De Geographia*, V, 4, viii (tr. H.L. Jones).
3 *Quaestiones naturales*, VI *(De terrae motu)*.
4 *Punica*, XII, 152 ff. (tr. J.D. Duff).
5 *Aeneid*, III, 578 ff.
6 'Le Corricolo' (in *Impressions de voyage*, 1845). Paris, 1872, II, 277-78.
7 *Aeneid*, II, 12.
8 A German physician, Dr Kantorowicz, has diagnosed the cause of Pliny's death as 'heart attack resulting from advanced coronary sclerosis'.
9 *Argonautica*, III, 208 ff. and IV, 507 ff.
10 *Mémoire sur le Vésuve*, November 30, 1739.
11 *Silvae*, V, 3.
12 *De Pythiae oraculis*, IV (tr. F.C. Babbitt).
13 The graffito, now lost, was discovered by Mau in August 1885, in Regio IX, Insula 1, 26.
14 Regio I, Insula 7, 1.
15 Regio VI, Insula 17, 7.

Bibliography

Alfano, G.B. and Friedlaender, I. *Die Geschichte des Vesuv*. Reimer, Berlin, 1929; Boissier, G. *Promenades archéologiques, Rome et Pompéi*. Hachette, Paris, 1913; Brion, M. *Pompeii and Herculaneum*. Elek Books, London, 1960; Van Buren, A.W. *A Companion to the Study of Pompeii and Herculaneum*. American Academy, Rome, 1933; *Pompeji*, article in Pauly-Wissowa, *Realenzyklopädie der klassischen Altertumswissenschaft* (Metzler, Stuttgart); Carcopino, J. *Etudes d'histoire chrétienne*. Albin Michel, Paris, 1953; Carrington, R.C. *Pompeii*. Clarendon Press, Oxford, 1936; Della Corte, M. *Case ed abitanti di Pompei*. Pompeii, 1954; Maiuri, A. *Introduzione alla studio di Pompei*. Pironti, Napoli, 1949; *Pompei.* (5th ed.), De Agostini, Novara, 1956; Mau, A. *Pompeji in Leben und Kunst*. Engelmann, Leipzig, 1900; Overbeck, J.A. *Pompeji in seinen Gebäuden, Altertümern und Kunstwerken*. Engelmann, Leipzig, 1884; Sergejenko, M.J. *Pompeji* (aus dem Russischen übers. v. M. Diehl). Kochler & Amelang, Leipzig, 1953; Sogliano, A. *Pompei nel suo sviluppo storico*. Athenaeum, Roma, 1937; Thédenat, A. *Pompéi—histoire, vie privée*. Laurens, Paris, 1906; *Pompéi—vie publique*. Laurens, Paris, 1906.

Chapter 2

Notes

1 Sir Nathaniel W. Wraxall, *Historical Memoirs of my own Time* (Philadelphia, 1845), 95.
2 *Tagebücher*, entry for May 19, 1849 (F.H. *Sämtliche Werke* [Berlin, 1905], II. Abt., III, 340).
3 De Brosses, *Lettres familières etc.* (Paris, n.d.), I, 360.
4 *Ibid.* 379, 383, 384.
5 The quotation is from Statius' *Silvae* (IV, 4).
6 *Gray and his Friends* (Letters etc. ed. by Duncan C. Tovey [Cambridge, 1890]), 252 ff.
7 F.W. v. Erdmannsdorff to Huber, 1766 (J.J.W., *Briefe* [ed. Diepolder-Rehm, Berlin, 1952-57), IV, 249.

8 *Briefe*, IV, 243. For Boswell's impression, see *Boswell on the Grand Tour (Italy, Corsica and France)*, entry for May 9, 1765.

9 To F.W. v. Schlabbrendorff, 1765 *(Briefe*, III, 127–128).

10 J.J. Volkmann's *Historisch-kritische Nachrichten von Italien etc.* (1770 and 1778), which in turn was indebted to Lalande's *Voyage d'un François en Italie* of 1769, and J.H. v. Riedesel's *Reise durch Sizilien und Grossgriechenland* (1771), which was to be translated into English and augmented by Sir William Hamilton.

11 According to Francesco La Vega's journal, the Herculanean Gate ('the city gate') had been discovered on September 14, 1763 and the surrounding area cleared that same year. The priestess' tomb is that of Mamia, with the inscription *Mamiae P.F. sacerdoti publicae locus sepulturae datus decurionum decreto* ('By public decree, this place was given as burial ground to Mamia, municipal priestess, daughter of Publius').

12 'The Innocents Abroad' (*The Writings of Mark Twain* [New York and London, 1906], II, 38).

13 *Spaziergang nach Syrakus im Jahre 1802* (Berlin, n.d.), II, 70.

14 A few years after this visit, Goethe reviewed Zahn's *Die schönsten Ornamente und merkwürdigsten Gemälde aus Pompeji, Herkulaneum und Stabiae* of 1828–30.

Bibliography

Acton, H. *The Bourbons of Naples*. Methuen, London, 1957; Allen, B.S. *Tides in English Taste*. Harvard University Press, 1937; Hatfield, H. *Winckelmann and his German Critics 1775–81*. Columbia University Press, New York, 1943; *Aesthetic Paganism in German Literature*. Harvard University Press, 1964; Justi, C. *Winckelmann und seine Zeitgenossen* (5th ed., ed. W. Rehm, 3 vols.). Phaidon, Köln, 1956; Ketton-Cremer, R.W. *Thomas Gray*. Cambridge University Press, 1955; v. Klenze, C. *The Interpretation of Italy during the Last Two Centuries* ('A Contribution to the Study of Goethe's *Italienische Reise*'). University of Chicago Press, 1907; Lewis, W.S. *Horace Walpole*. Pantheon, New York, 1960; Manwaring, E. *Italian Landscape in Eighteenth-Century England*. Oxford University Press, New York, 1925; Marshall, R. *Italy in English Literature, 1755–1815*. Columbia University Press, 1934; Murga, F.F. *Los ingenieros españoles R.J. de Alcubierre y F. La Vega, descubridores de Herculano, Pompeya y Estabia*. Facultad de Filosofía y Letras, Madrid, 1964; Rostovtsev, M.I. *Mystic Italy*. Holt, New York, 1927; Roe, F.C. *Le voyage de Gray et Walpole en Italie* (in *Revue de littérature comparée*, April–June 1926 [Paris]); Rüdiger, H. *Winckelmann und Italien*. Scherpe, Krefeld, 1956; Trevelyan, H. *Goethe and the Greeks*. Cambridge University Press, 1941.

Chapter 3

Notes

1 Herold, 312; Gennari, 10.

2 *Corinne; or, Italy* (tr. by E. Baldwin & P. Driver [London, 1888]), 203.

3 *Lettres familières*, etc., I, 308.

4 Chateaubriand's *Lettre à M. de Fontanes* and Bonstetten's *Voyage sur la scène des six derniers livres de l'Eneide* had been published in 1804.

5 'Voyage en Italie' *(Oeuvres complètes de Chateaubriand*, Paris, n.d.), VI, 301.

6 *Le gardien de Pompéi*, in *Du Vésuve à l'Etna* (Paris, 1952).

7 *Œuvres complètes de Lamartine* (Paris, 1863), XXIX, 219 and 196.

8 Mattlé, 55 and 59.

9 Regio VIII, Insula 2, 1–5.

10 Lehmann, 8.

11 Acton, xvi.

12 Lehmann, 26.

13 Origo, 249.
14 Vossler, 357.

Bibliography

Acton, H. *The Last Bourbons of Naples*. Methuen, London, 1961; Bisi, A. *L'Italie et le romantisme français*. Albrighi, Segati & Co., Milano, 1914; Blennerhasset, Lady (Comtesse de Leyden). *Madame de Staël et son temps*. Westhausser, Paris, 1890; Brand, C.P. *Italy and the English Romantics*. Cambridge University Press, 1957; Cenzatti, G. *Alfonso de Lamartine e l'Italia*. Giusti, Livorno, 1903; Gennari, G. *Le premier voyage de Madame de Staël et la genèse de Corinne*. Boivin, Paris, n.d.; Häusler, R. *Das Bild Italiens in der deutschen Romantik*. Haupt, Bern/Leipzig, 1939; Hazard, P. *Stendhal et l'Italie* (in *Revue des deux mondes*, 1 & 15 Dec. 1926 and 15 Jan. 1927 [Paris]); Herold, J.C. *Mistress to an Age* (A Life of Madame de Staël). Bobbs-Merrill, Indianapolis/New York, 1958; Lehmann, J. *Shelley in Italy*. Purnell & Sons, London, 1947; Mattlé, R. *Lamartine voyageur*. De Boccard, Paris, 1936; Mengin, U. *L'Italie des romantiques*. Librairie Plon, Paris, 1902; *Lamartine à Naples et à Ischia* (in *Revue de littérature comparée*, Oct.-Dec. 1924 [Paris]); Noli, R. *Les romantiques français et l'Italie*. Bernigaud & Privat, Dijon, 1928; Origo, I. *Leopardi*. Hamish Hamilton, London, 1953; Porta, M. *Madame de Staël e l'Italia*. Ferranti-Gonnelli, Firenze, 1909; Vossler, K. *Leopardi*. (2nd ed.), Karl Winter, Heidelberg, 1930.

Chapter 4
Notes

1 Preface to the Edition of 1834', where Bulwer also acknowledges his debt to Sir Walter Scott.
2 Sir William Gell, or, possibly, Antonio Bonucci.
3 *Italie et Sicile*, in *Course en voiturin* (Paris, 1845).
4 S.B. Liljegren, *Bulwer-Lytton's Novels and Isis Unveiled* (Upsala-Lund, 1957).
5 H. Füssli to H.C. Vögelin, 1764.
6 Joncs, II, 341.
7 *Der Wahn und die Träume in W. Jensens 'Gradiva'* (2nd ed., Leipzig/Wien, 1912), 42–43.
8 Letter to Jung, May 26, 1907.
9 In an article on 'Freud a Pompeii', in the *Mattino* of Naples, October 28, 1962.
10 Musatti, 232.

Bibliography

Bell, E.G. *Introductions to the Prose Romances, Plays, and Comedies of Edward Bulwer Lord Lytton*. Hill, Chicago, 1914; Du Camp, M. *Théophile Gautier*. Hachette, Paris, n.d.; Costigan, G. *Sigmund Freud*. Macmillan, New York & London, 1965; Freud, S. *Briefe 1873–1939* (ausgew. u. herausgegeben von E.L. Freud). S. Fischer, Frankfurt, 1960; Jones, E. *The Life and Works of Sigmund Freud*. 3 vols., Basic Books, New York, 1953–57; Lytton, Earl of. *The Life of Edward Bulwer, First Lord Lytton*. 2 vols., Macmillan, London, 1913; Musatti, C.L. *Gradiva, un racconto di Wilhelm Jensen e uno studio analitico di Sigmund Freud*. Boringhieri, Torino, 1961; Pabst, W. 'Venus und die missverstandene Dido' (*Literarische Ursprünge des Sibyllen- und des Venusberges*). Cram, de Gruyter & Co., Hamburg, 1955; Palache, J.G. *Gautier and the Romantics*. Jonathan Cape, London, 1927; Praz, M. *La carne, la morte e il diavolo nella letteratura romantica*. 3. ed., Sansoni, Firenze, 1948; Sadler, M. 'Edward and Rosina' (Part I of *Bulwer: A Panorama*). Little, Brown & Co., Boston, 1931; Sheppard, A.T. *The Art and Practice of Historical Fiction*. Humphrey Toulmin, London, 1930.

Chapter 5

Notes

1 *Italian Sights and Papal Principles* (New York, 1856), 174.
2 *Pencillings by the Way* (Philadelphia, 1836), 57, and *Italian Journeys* (Boston, 1893), 89.
3 *Journal of a Visit to Europe and the Levant* (Princeton, 1955), 176.
4 *Japanese Lady in Europe* (New York, 1937), 330, and 'Present Estate of Pompeii' (in *Hear us O Lord from heaven thy dwelling place*, Philadelphia & New York, 1961), 185.
5 Waldstein, 196.
6 S. Münz, in *Neue Freie Presse* (Vienna), September 27, 1906.
7 Acton, *The Last Bourbons of Naples* (London, 1961), 476.
8 K.P. Moritz, *Reisen eines Deutschen in Italien in den Jahren 1786 bis 1788* (Berlin, 1792–93), II, 61–62.
9 'La ciudad resucitada', in *En el país del arte* (Madrid, ed. of 1961), I, 219.
10 *Pompeii*, in *Meyer's Universum* (Hildburghausen, 1859).
11 *Das Gesamtwerk* (Frankfurt, 1959), 89.

Bibliography

Beall, C., Eugenio Montale's 'Sarcofaghi', in *Linguistic and Literary Studies in Honour of Helmut A. Hatzfeld*. Catholic University of America Press, Washington, 1964; Brooks, V.W., 'The Dream of Arcadia' (*American Writers and Artists in Italy, 1760–1915*). Dutton, New York, 1958; Charpentier, J., *Alexandre Dumas*, Tallandier, Paris, 1947; Corti, E.C. Conte, *Untergang und Auferstehung von Pompeji und Herkulaneum*. 7. ed., Bruckmann, München, 1951; De Franciscis, A., *Il ritratto romano a Pompei*. Macchiaroli, Napoli, 1951; *Il museo nazionale di Napoli*. Di Mauro, Cava dei Tirreni, 1963; Grossman, J., *James Fenimore Cooper*. Wm. Sloane Associates, New York, 1949; Johnson, E., *Charles Dickens. His Tragedy and Triumph*. 2 vols., Gollancz, London, 1953; Maiuri, A., *Taccuino Napoletano*. Vajro, Napoli, 1956; Paine, A.B., *Mark Twain*. 3 vols., Harper & Bros., New York/London, 1912; Prezzolini, G., *Come gli americani scoprirono l'Italia* (1750–1850). Treves, Milano, 1933; Waldstein, C., and Shoobridge, L., *Herculaneum— Past, Present, and Future*. London, 1908.

Index